HARDPRESS.NET
HOME OF HARD-TO-FIND BOOKS

Elements of the Veterinary Art
by Charles Vial De Sainbel

Address:
HardPress
8345 NW 66TH ST #2561
MIAMI FL 33166-2626
USA
Email: info@hardpress.net

CHARLES VICTOR DE SILLERY,

ELEMENTS

OF THE

VETERINARY ART,

CONTAINING

AN ESSAY

ON THE PROPORTIONS OF THE CELEBRATED ECLIPSE;

SIX LECTURES ON FARRIERY,

OR THE ART OF HORSE-SHOEING,

AND ON THE DISEASES OF THE FOOT.

AN ESSAY ON THE GREASE,

WHICH OBTAINED THE PRIZE GIVEN BY THE ROYAL SOCIETY OF MEDICINE.

AN ESSAY ON THE GLANDERS;

AND OBSERVATIONS ON THE GRIPES.

The whole illustrated with Nine Anatomical, Geometrical, and Mechanical Engravings.

BY

CHARLES VIAL DE SAINBEL,

LATE EQUERRY TO THE KING, AND PROFESSOR TO THE VETERINARY COLLEGE.

To which is prefixed,
A SHORT ACCOUNT OF HIS LIFE.

THE THIRD EDITION.

LONDON:
PRINTED FOR J. WRIGHT, 169, PICCADILLY.

1797.

dour, bordering upon enthusiasm, for its improvement.

He stands the corner- stone and original source of that knowledge and practice which is now adopting in London ; and diffusing itself throughout this kingdom, respecting the proper method of treating *the horse* in every stage of *its* diseases and infirmities. 'Till his residence in England, *true veterinary science* was unknown among us, although studied and practised in every other part of Europe. To remedy this defect in some measure, the *Odiham Society* (for the encouragement of agriculture, &c.) had it in contemplation to send two young men from this country into France, to study in one of the schools there. The motive appears to have been not only to introduce a judicious mode for the treatment of horses and other cattle into this kingdom, but also to extend this science and its practice. Patriotic and humane as was the plan, yet from so confined an effort little more than a local and partial advantage could

could be hoped for : it is to be feared such a beginning would have had but a small chance of success, from the opposition naturally arising in old and long-rooted prejudices.

Happily, however, for this kingdom, and the beautiful stock of cattle it produces, the mission of these young men into France was prevented by the arrival of Mons. de Sainbel, who just at this period, took up his residence in England. The very judicious manner in which he dissected the body of ECLIPSE, (a horse at once our glory and our pride, from his unequalled and unrivalled powers) and the proofs he daily gave of his knowledge in the veterinary science, soon gained him the patronage of many noblemen * and gentlemen ; from the zeal of one of whom, assisted by a few others, and his own exertions, arose THE VETERINARY COLLEGE OF LONDON ; an institution of the

* The right honourable Earl Grosvenor and Earl Morton were his most early and distinguished patrons.

the greatest consequence to this nation ; and which, (though at present struggling with some untoward difficulties,) will, no doubt, in time equal, if not rival, the other veterinary seminaries of Europe, not only by the excellence of its practice, and the consequent information convey-ed to the pupils who are admitted to study there ; but by the perpetual source of knowledge it will disseminate throughout the kingdom, producing the greateſt benefit to most of those animals de-stined to the domestic use of man.

Having thus introduced the author of the fol-lowing works to the attention of my readers, I shall now proceed to give a narrative of his life, partly from the manuscripts he has left in the hands of his widow ; as also from my own obser-vations and knowledge, assisted by the informa-tion I have received from those who much es-teemed him.

Mons.

Mons. Vial de Sainbel was born at Lyons, January 28th, 1753; at which time his grand father held the important office of mayor; this family having been long possessed of a domaine in that province, called Sainbel, they added this cognomen to that of VIAL (as was the case through-out France before the Revolution of 1789.) At three years old, he lost his grand father and both his parents; his father having appointed Mons. de Flesseille to be his guardian, this gentleman very kindly took him under his care; with him he remained till he was sixteen: at which age, being impelled by his great propensity for investigating the organization of animals, he went one day to the Veterinary School to see its museum: After satisfying his curiosity, he requested an interview with the professor, Mons. Pêan; of this gentleman he solicited permission to attend the lectures as an out-pupil; which, being contrary to the rules of the college, he was refused; but he obtained leave to become a student at his own expence; this in a few days

c   he

he accomplished. On his being entered, he was introduced not only to the study of the outward conformation of the horse, but also to that of the cutaneous diseases of the legs: which, being congenial to his wishes, he applied so closely, that in a short space of time he gained the prize alotted to the best essay on the grease, being the subject of discussion for the day. *

His patron, guardian, and friend, Mons. de Flesseille, was so much pleased with this progress of young Sainbel, that he soon after gratified him with an annuity of 500 livres, not only as a reward and encouragement, but also as an earnest of his future favours. By these marks of public approbation and private patronage, he was impelled to greater exertions, and more intense application, so that at the end of two years he obtained the appointment of lecturer and demonstrator to a class of sixteen of the pupils; the next year

* This Essay makes a part of the present Volume.

year he was made upper student, assistant surgeon, and one of the public demonstrators, a situation of great importance, on account of its extensive practice, and the opportunity it afforded of obtaining patrons. He had not been in this charge above twelve months before a dreadful epizootic disorder broke out among the horses, in many of the provinces of France. Upon the frequent and pressing representations made of this destructive calamity to the Veterinary College at Lyons, he was ordered to chuse five students out of it to accompany him in his provincial visits, in order to assist in stopping the ravages of this evil. This mission was so compleatly accomplished, that on his return, he brought with him the most ample official testimonials of his skill, from the places where he had thus fortunately practiced.

Soon after his return to Lyons, he was sent for to Paris by the late king's express orders, and appointed one of the junior professorial assistants to the Royal Veterinary College. Thus raised,

ed,

ed, he endeavoured to fulfil the duties of this station by every exertion that a gratified and grateful mind could inspire.

But here (as if fortune was wearied in bestowing her favours upon him) arose an unexpected opposition to his progress, from the jealousy of one of the professors. This man finding that M. Sainbel was gaining, by his skill and assiduity, a great ascendency not only over the minds of the students, but of some of the directors, whose dispositions led them to a right judgment of, and attention to, real merit : and fearing that by his means many of the old and absurd methods of practice still adhered to, would be exploded, and œconomical abuses rectified (by which some of the adherents to the old school might lose not only their consequence, but their situations), he was determined to nip him in the bud. He, therefore, urged M. Chabert and others, in the direction, to enter into a scheme, not only to humble M. Sainbel, but to bring him into that state of submission and silence that
would,

would, in future, keep him under their controul and mandates; for this purpose he wrote the following note:

" My dear friend, and brother professor, Chabert,
   " I need not again remind you of our present
" irksome situation---this young headstrong, of
" inflexible manners, renders our condition both
" disagreeable and unsafe. What do you think
" of his conduct the day before yesterday, at the
" public lecture? Ought he not to have praised,
" instead of attempted to prove me a plagiarist
" and quack. I own that I previously treated him
" *en cavalier.* What, then? Was I not his se-
" nior, and should he not have taken it in good
" part, and as an honour done him, to be in
" *any manner* noticed? But no---he chose to re-
" tort and insult my abilities. It must be allow-
" ed that he has merit, and has acquired some-
" thing like skill; but his practice is so novel,
" that we must either give up ours, or he must
" his. We professors, have had (you know, my
                          " dear

" dear Chabert) so *perfect* an understanding with
" each other, throughout the whole college, that
" if one of us *was found* not quite so illumined on
" certain subjects as could be wished, each of us
" winked in our turn at it, and all has been *kept*
" right. Confer with Sainbel as soon as you can :
" get at his private opinion, not only of me but
" of our colleagues ; and try to bend him to our
" views. If you find him inflexibly determined
" upon his system of novelty and œconomy,---we
" must crush him.

" You know my interest with the minister. I
" will immediately after your conference (if he re-
" mains obstinate) represent him to be not only a
" wrong-headed, troublesome and dangerous fel-
" low, but also an enemy to all order, and disaf-
" fected to good government, (I do not say what
" government. I leave the minister to *construe*
" that ; and as he is most likely to take the word
" in its wrong sense, by his so doing, I get rid
" of all responsibility.) I shall conclude my
" appli-

" application by soliciting his removal from
" hence. A letter de cachet will issue, and
" the *Bastile* (from whence he shall never return)
" be the dernier theatre demonstratif of Mons.
" our petit professeur en second. I am, with all
" sincerity of attachment and esteem,

"My dear professor,

" Your's,

" BOURGELAT."

The premeditated injustice so apparent in this
letter operated with such force on Chabert's confi-
dential pupil, who had contracted an intimacy
with, and a sincere esteem for M. Sainbel, that he
not only communicated its contents to him, but
also furnished him with a copy of it ;* and Sainbel, well knowing the vindictive spirit of
Bourgelat, Chabert, and their adherents, and that
the safest way for him was to give in his resigna-
tion ;

* As it is from this source the Editor has translated so singular a production, he leaves the candid and discerning Reader to form such a judgment
thereon as he thinks fit ; he can only say it was found among the late Mr.
Sainbel's papers, and that it appeared of too much consequence to be left out
in this biographical sketch of his life.

tion; he instantly did so. Having obtained
his congé, he quitted Paris, and returned to Lyons, the place of his nativity and of his former happiness: there he practised as a veterinary physician and surgeon for some time;
but being disappointed in forming an alliance
(by marriage) with a lady for whom he had
long entertained an affection, he returned to
Paris, at the request of Mons. de St. Priest, then,
governor of Languedoc, and one of his warm patrons; a short time after his arrival, being informed by this nobleman, that the demonstrator
of comparative anatomy to the Veterinary College
of Montpelier was dead, and that if he chose to
accept of this situation, it was at his service; he
readily assented to the offer, and went to that
city, where he was appointed anatomical professor; in this office he remained five years (the
time for which he engaged himself to it) at the
expiration whereof, he revisited Paris, being
sent for by the Prince de Lambesc, another of his
patrons; with this nobleman he remained three
                                      years,

years, during which he was made one of the
equerries to the king (Louis XVI.) and chief of the
manage of the academy of Lyons : the latter of
which he held some years with great gratification
to his mind, as he thereby could indulge, at
times, his favourite researches in veterinary study,
as well as that of horsemanship; in which latter
he also was a very great proficient. It was during
this period that he used many efforts to be restored
to his former situation in the Royal Veterinary
College of Paris, but being disappointed, he was
determined, by the advice of Mr. Brousonet, to
accomplish the design he had long entertained of
visiting England; for this purpose, he obtained
six months leave of absence ; and having received
letters of introduction to Sir Joseph Banks, Dr.
Simmons, Dr. Layard of Greenwich, and other
respectable characters in this kingdom, he arrived here in June 1788 ; in September following he published proposals for instituting a Ve-
erinary School, but without success. Having, during this first visit, married an English lady of great
accomplishments, he returned with her to Paris ;

but finding, after some time, that discontents and factious habits of thinking, with respect to national matters, were extending themselves rapidly in that city, and throughout France, he obtained leave to revisit England, under the pretext of purchasing horses for his sovereign's stud : fortunately for him (so far as relates to his existence) but more so for this kingdom, he was in this country at the breaking out of the revolution and the destruction of the Bastile.   In this first commotion he lost his guardian and friend, Mons. de Flesseille, who fell the second victim to that unjust, indiscriminate vengeance, of an enraged people.   By the death of this great and good man, he lost his annuity of 500 livres.   By the restraint exercised over his monarch, and by the death or emigration of his other great friends, he was shortly after deprived of the offices he held; and lastly, his patrimonial estate of Sainbel was confiscated, on account of his being deemed an emigrant, by not returning to France within the time prescribed by the then demagogues who had obtained the executive government thereof.

Thus circumstanced, he was determined to make England the place of his future residence; he took his measures accordingly; and in February following, being requested by Mr. O'Kelly to dissect the body of that wonderful horse, Eclipse; he displayed such great and unusual talents (as a veterinary anatomist) that it soon gained him not only the highest reputation, but many noble and zealous patrons. In the year 1790, he again endeavoured to attract the notice of the public to his views, namely of founding a school to instruct pupils, veterinary medicine, and surgery. His plan was now so well received, that the Odiham Society, for the improvement of agriculture, &c. not only gave up the idea and intention of sending their two young men into France; but they made him an honorary member of their body; from which they delegated a committee of gentlemen to confer with him respecting the aforesaid plan, and whatever might tend to the improvement of farriery, and also of the proper treatment of other cattle in this kingdom. This

D 2

com-

committee being joined by some gentlemen` in
London, they resolved to invite the public **to**
their conferences ; having advertised their **in-**
tentions, and that their meeting would be **held**
the 11th of the next month (February 1**791**)
at the Blenheim coffee-house, in Bond-**street,**
they were that evening attended by a few **in-**
dividuals, who being admitted members **of this**
infant society, the following declaration **and**
resolution was passed.

THAT " this meeting, highly sensible **of the**
" great benefit that must result to this king**dom**
" from an institution to cultivate and **teach**
" veterinary medicine and surgery therein, **and**
" also of the plan proposed to them by **Mons.**
" Vial de Sainbel (in the views and utili**ty of**
" which they fully coincide) ; they, ther**efore,**
" RESOLVE that a committee, consisting of **four**
" gentlemen be requested to confer with **him,**
" and to consolidate, if possible, their inte**ntions**
" with his views."

On

On the 18th of the same month (being the adjourned meeting of the society, after the admission of some very respectable members) GRANVILLE PENN, ESQ. the Chairman informed them that their committee had conferred with M. Sainbel, who had not only explained and proved the utility and practicability of his plan, but that he had also offered to unite his efforts to those of the society; it was in consequence

RESOLVED,

" That this society do forthwith inform the
" gentlemen of Odiham, THAT, from the ac-
" cess of a great many members, resident in Lon-
" don, and for other local and cogent reasons,
" they mean to detach themselves from their
" body, and form an institution to be called the
" VETERINARY COLLEGE OF LONDON.
" at the same time requesting their friendly inter-
" course and aid. Resolved also, that Mons. Vial
" de Sainbel should be requested to accept the
" professorship to the said Veterinary College."

The

The number of subscribers daily increasing, a general meeting was called the 8th of April, when the following noblemen and gentlemen were chosen president, vice-presidents, and directors,

PRESIDENT.

HIS GRACE THE DUKE OF NORTHUMBERLAND.

VICE-PRESIDENTS

EARL GROSVENOR,
EARL MORTON,
EARL OF OXFORD,
LORD RIVERS,
SIR GEORGE BAKER, BART.
SIR J. C. BUNBURY, BART. M. P.
SIR WM. FORDYCE, KNT. AND
JOHN HUNTER, ESQ.

DIRECTORS.

SIR JOHN INGILBY, BART. M. P.
SIR H. P. ST. JOHN MILDMAY, BART.
G. M. ASCOUGH, ESQ.
MR. J. BAYNES,
F. J. BROWNE, ESQ. M. P
MR. J. BURGESS,
REV. T. BURGESS,
REV. J. COOK,

DR.

DR. ADAIR CRAWFORD,
JOHN GRETTON, ESQ.
DR. HAMILTON,
MR. KENNETT,
DR. D. MAPLETON,
GRANVILLE PENN, ESQ.
MR. WM. STONE,
EDWARD TOPHAM, ESQ.
DR. WILLIAMS, AND
J. WOLLASTON, ESQ.

Messieurs Ransom, Morland, and Hammersly were appointed Treasurers, and M. de Sainbel was confirmed in his nomination of Professor.

The 3d of May following, the constitution, with its rules and orders, was partly settled and published. At this meeting, a letter from the Odiham Society was read, expressing their satisfaction at the success of, and their good wishes for, the Veterinary College of London; and that as a testimony thereof, they had directed their secretary to send up to the said college all such papers as they were possessed of respecting veterinary matters; and further, that they had directed

rected him to request of the subscribers to their veterinary fund, the transfer of their subscriptions to the assistance of this society.

On the 22d March, 1792, it was resolved, that a *temporary* stabling for fifty horses, and a forge house for shoeing, should be built on a piece of ground, near Pancras, which had been previously taken for the use of this institution.

On the 26th April following, it was resolved, at the request of the professor, (to do away any doubt as to his abilities or character, he being a foreigner) That a committee, consisting of Sir George Baker, Dr. Crawford, and Dr. Packwood, together with Mr. John Hunter, Mr. Cline, Mr. Home, Mr. Vaux, Mr. Sheldon, and Mr. Peake, be desired to examine M. de Sainbel, as to his qualifications in veterinary medicine and surgery; and that Earl Morton, Lord Heathfield, and some other noblemen and gentlemen, be requested

quested to examine the documents and other proofs of his mode of conduct while resident in France.

After due investigation, the committees made their respective reports as follows : The medical and surgical committee report, IT is perfectly satisfied that Mr. Sainbel is in every respect qualified for the office of veterinary professor to the college of London: and Earl Morton, from the committee of which he was president, reported, That it is perfectly satisfied with the character and conduct of the professor, Mons. Sainbel.

From this time, until the above gentleman's death, the institution gained ground most rapidly, notwithstanding its being involved in great pecuniary embarrassments, from expensive buildings, and an ill-judged system adopted by some persons in the direction of its funds.

" *Hinc ille lachrymæ! !* * * * * * * * * * * *

* * * * * * * * * * * * * * * * * * * *

E   Arrived

Arrived now at that period of biography the most painful to the mind of a friend and an historian, I mean the detail of that melancholy event which so early deprived the institution of its first professor, its great support and firm friend. I shall be as brief as possible, for the sake of my own feelings, as well as of those by whom he was esteemed, in stating, that it was on Sunday the 4th of August 1793, after having finished the morning duty he always performed in person, of visiting, prescribing for, and superintending the dressing of, the wounds of the horses in the infirmary, that he sat down to continue his treatise on the outward conformation of the horse, a work he intended for publication ; in a short time he informed Mrs. Sainbel that he felt himself extremely ill, complaining of cold to a degree of shivering, attended with a violent head-ach, and great thirst. She administered to him some wine diluted with warm water. By this, finding himself relieved, he again resumed his studies till the hour of dinner, when the disorder again attacked

attacked him so violently that it produced a fainting fit, which held him till the evening ; he went soon after to bed, and passed a very uneasy, restless night. The next day Dr. Crawford was called to him. Under the care of this gentleman he remained near a week ; when, not finding that relief he hoped for, Dr. Scott was requested to assist Dr. Crawford, but with no better success, for, notwithstanding the united efforts of these eminent physicians, the fever and faintings encreased till they ended in a delirium and death on the 21st, being seventeen days after the first attack.

Thus ended the life of this assiduous and skilful veterinarian, who had just entered the 40th year of his age. His body lies interred at the expence of the College (as a tribute to his memory) in the vault of the Savoy Chapel in the Strand.

If I may be permitted to bring my praise-offering to his shrine, I shall say he was a

man

man of the nicest honour; impatient of every thing that tended to obstruct or suspend the success of the institution over which he presided as professor. Thus zealously attached, he felt much regret on the death or secession of some of its first friends and founders; in consequence of which he struggled (with unremitting exertions) to prevent the effects which unavoidably resulted therefrom; and that these efforts, joined to the anxieties he suffered respecting the fate of his native country France, together with the melancholy situation of his late sovereign and master, weighed so heavy upon his spirits, that he fell a martyr to them.

Had he lived till now, many of the mortifications which he experienced would have ceased, his hopes been encouraged, his wishes gratified, (and in my humble opinion his days prolonged) by the aid he would have received from the exertions of those noblemen and gentlemen who have lately taken upon them to correct former

errors

errors by substituting liberal economy in the place of that delusive speculation, which has proved so injurious to the success of the institution.

Soon after his death, at a general meeting of the subscribers to the institution, an annuity of 6ol. was generously granted to his widow; this mark of kindness they have been obliged to recall, from the present precarious income of the college. To remedy in some degree this severe blow upon her happiness and subsistence, the Editor has undertaken the task of compiling this memoir; and of publishing this volume, consisting of some of the veterinary productions of her late husband; the profits of which he means to dedicate to her, whose infancy he admired and respected, and whose present situation he very much deplores.

AN

ESSAY

ON THE

PROPORTIONS

OF

ECLIPSE.

BY

CHARLES VIAL DE SAINBEL,

LATE EQUERRY TO THE KING, AND PROFESSOR TO THE VETERINARY COLLEGE.

THIRD EDITION.

LONDON:

PRINTED FOR

J. WRIGHT, 169, PICCADILLY.

1797.

ADVERTISEMENT.

W HEN I first employed myself in taking the proportions of Eclipse, I had no other object in view, than to gratify my own curiosity with respect to the figure, extent, and direction of the parts which compose a race-horse, and to compare them with those of horses of different kinds, for the purpose of informing myself of the mechanical causes which conspire to augment the velocity of the gallop; of course, the Essay which I here offer contains only some general ideas on the mechanism of the organs of progression. I will, however, venture to affirm, that these ideas are capable of being extended, and may conduce to the knowledge of the mechanical causes of the *translation* * of every animated machine. The

bones,

---

* The word *translation* signifies the removal, or conveying of the body forward, by its natural powers; and is borrowed from the original, on account of its simplicity of expression.

bones and muscles exhibit an apparatus of columns, levers, pullies, cords, wedges, &c. whose
combined operations effect the removal of the
body with greater or less speed.　The knowledge
of these parts is therefore necessary for forming a
judgment of the motions of the horse, of their
origin, capacity, extent, succession, &c.　This
knowledge is not less necessary to those artists
who design to represent the animal upon canvass,
or in marble.　The painter or statuary, who stops
at the surface of the parts, can never give a just
representation of the truth ; he must carry his
enquiries beyond the outward case, which conceals the causes of the motions which he wishes
to express.　Since it is true, that the construction and direction of the bony and muscular parts
within determine the outward figure of the body,
a table of proportions, collected from the best
race-horses, would be of great service.　1st. As a
surer guide to the brush or chisel of the artist,
who commonly only employs them in opposition
to nature.　2d. It would teach a better choice of
the

the animal, and to exact from it no greater exertions than Nature had rendered it capable of yielding. 3d. By means of this table we should be enabled to establish the true conformation of the race-horse ; and at any given time to discover whether the breed had improved or degenerated. In short, I submit these observations to the Reader; and in the mean time shall employ myself in treating of the elements of Veterinary Medicine, for the use of the pupils of the newly-projected Veterinary College. If I can render myself any way useful to the Public, I shall have obtained the purpose of every good citizen.

AN
ESSAY
ON THE
PROPORTIONS
OF
ECLIPSE.

DEATH of ECLIPSE.

IN the morning of the 25th of February 1789 Eclipse was seized with a violent cholic. The remedies acknowledged as most proper in that case were administered, but without effect. He expired on the 27th, at seven o'clock in the evening, in the 26th year of his age.

Opening

Opening of the Body.

THE opening of the abdomen, or lower belly, presented immediately an overflowing of sanguinous serum ; all the intestines were in a state of extreme inflammation, and even covered over with gangrenous spots. The mesentery and the epiploon were in the same condition ; the glands appeared much swelled, and the blood-vessels were filled with a black thick blood, apparently without any serum. The stomach was entirely empty ; its inward membrane little inflamed ; the spleen was much obstructed, as was also the liver, one lobe of which was partly in a state of putrefaction. The dissection of the reins, or kidnies, more particularly discovered the cause of the disease ; the pelvis was filled with purulent matter, and the membranes completely destroyed by the effect of suppuration. The bladder did not contain a drop of urine, but only a certain quantity of pus, conveyed by the ureters ; its villous coat was corroded by the matter. From the above stances I infer, that the reins performed their functions in a very imperfect manner, and that the animal died in consequence of the affections of these viscera, and of a violent inflammation in the bowels. The viscera of the chest partook, in a very slight degree, of this inflammation. It is worthy notice, that the heart weighed fourteen pounds. The skull was not opened, as it was my intention to preserve entire the skeleton of so famous a horse.

Comparative Remarks between the Proportions of
ECLIPSE, and the Table of the Geometrical Pro-
portions of the Horse in the Use of the Pupils of the
Veterinary Schools of France.

THE horses of different countries
are in general distinguished from each other by a
peculiar, appropriate conformation. The Spanish
horse differs materially in his outward appearance from the English race-horse. The difference in the length and direction of the parts of
which each is composed produces in each a system, from whose mechanic arrangement result
motions very unequal in their extent. The Spanish horse cadences his steps with dignity, while
the English horse drives his mass forward with
strength and speed. This difference, which proceeds from the peculiar conformation of each,
contradicts in some particulars the table of geometrical proportions in the use of the pupils of
the Veterinary Schools of France. It proves,
that

that no common measure can be made to apply equally to every species, since Nature has even diversified the forms of the individuals which compose it.

If each species has its own style of beauty; if even each individual has its own peculiar beauty; if it is not possible to find two horses that perfectly resemble each other; we cannot pretend to assign any one form preferably to another, as the rule of beauty for the horse. Were persons the best qualified to endeavour to collect together the different beauties dispersed among the different individuals, they might indeed compose a model of each species sufficiently perfect to direct the painter or the statuary, but which would deceive any one who would venture to choose an horse by it for his own use. The following observations do not take for their object those forms which please the eye ·at the first glance, that appearance which vulgarly passes for hand-

C 2   some :

some : but that mechanical construction of the animal, from which result the possibility and extent of those motions by the means of which he is enabled to transport himself from one place to another with greater or less speed. And, consequently, an horse may appear ugly to a vulgar eye, and be still well proportioned. Eclipse was never esteemed handsome ; yet he was swift, and the mechanism of his frame almost perfect. Whoever compares his proportions with those in the table abovementioned will discover the following differences.

1st. In that table the horse should measure three heads in height, counting from the foretop to the ground. Eclipse measured upwards of three heads and an half.

2dly. The neck should measure but one head in length ; that of Eclipse measured an head and an half.

3dly.

3dly. The height of the body should be equal to its length; the height of Eclipse exceeded his length by about one tenth*.

4thly. A perpendicular line falling from the stifle should touch the toe; this line in Eclipse touched the ground at the distance of half an head before the toe.

5thly. The distance from the elbow to the bend of the knee, should be the same as from the bend of the knee to the ground; these two distances were unequal in Eclipse, the former being two parts of an head longer than the latter.

This summary comparison shews, that the beauty of the horse cannot be absolutely determined by general rules, but must ever be in relation to the particular species.

Although

---

* It must be observed, that the body of Eclipse is represented too short by two inches in the profile of the first plate, which fault is owing to the Engraver.

Although M. BOURGELAT has not given to his system all the extent which it was capable of receiving, we must nevertheless acknowledge, that the consequences which he deduces from it may, under certain modifications, serve to explain the mechanism of the different species of horses.

It is certain, that the different degrees of speed which we observe in the paces of horses of different kinds, result principally from the mechanic combination of the pieces which compose the organs of progression ; and it is only in examining their proportions when just, in ascertaining their exactness, their perpendicular, their absolute and relative directions, that we can conceive any hopes of apprehending the intentions and purposes of Nature.

Essay on the Geometrical Proportions of Eclipse.

ALTHOUGH it may be impossible for us to compute the natural strength of the muscles, we may nevertheless investigate the mechanical causes which operate the translation or removal of animal bodies, observe their effects, and come to some result concerning the difference of speed in the progression of different animals.

This requires, first, a knowledge of the anatomy and mechanism of the animal œconomy; secondly, a knowledge of the laws of motion ; by means of which we are enabled to calculate the causes and effects of the operations of which the animal is capable.

Since it is evident, that Nature has calculated and combined all her productions, and has subjected herself in general to the established laws of mechanics.;

mechanics; it is obvious, that we ought to apply
the lights which proceed from the knowledge of
these laws to the examination and illustration of
her works. It is only in disputing, as it were,
with her, in seeming to question her power, in
boldly attempting to remove the veil under which
she conceals herself, that we in a manner con-
strain her to explain herself upon an infinite variety of important points, on which ignorance
alone has hitherto ventured to pronounce.

It is not an habit imperceptibly acquired, nor
a vague routine, nor a practice unestablished on
sure principles, that can ever give us satisfactory
solutions of an infinity of problems, which Nature
presents daily to our attention; it is by the con-
stancy of study and reflection only, that we can
be enabled to establish new principles upon subjects which the light of science has never yet illumined.

It is sufficient to offer a new system, to acquire
both followers and opponents. The reflections

which I am going to hazard concerning the geometrical proportions of Eclipse, will, in all probability, offend some of the prejudices received
among the partizans of the turf; but if it should
be in my power to offer them any truths, I have
at least a claim upon their indulgence.

No one is ignorant that the course of progression
is not the same in all animals. The difference is
certainly very considerable between the slow and
tedious pace of the animal which we call the sloth,
and the velocity of the hare. But, without recurring for an instance to the two extremes of the
long chain of quadrupeds, I shall confine myself
to one in the species which at present concerns us.
Speed is not only unequal in animals of different
species, but even in individuals of the same. How
different, for example, is the gallop of a large
dray-horse from that of a good race-horse? It is
with difficulty that the former moves his body to
determine it into the pace required; he gathers
the ground heavily under him at each step, and

D

the

the translation of his bulk is but tardily effected. The latter, on the contrary, flies as an arrow from a bow, and scarcely imprints the ground with his shoe ; he often runs over a space of four miles in less than eight minutes. These are, however, but individuals of one and the same class. The number of the parts which conspire to effect their respective progression is the same in each : but these parts differ in their bulk, their extent, and their direction ; from whence result different degrees of power in the levers which they form. So that we are not to imagine that the mass or weight of the horse is the only cause of his slowness, which rather proceeds from the mechanical arrangement of the parts, whose relation and correspondence determine the extent of his motions.

The extent of the action of any part is the produce of its length and direction. The force of the action is rather the consequence of the direction of the muscles, than of their intrinsic power ;

power, which must unavoidably vary, being increased or diminished, in proportion as the muscles are more or less removed from the centre or
axis of the parts which they are to move. It will
be necessary to illustrate this principle. Let us
then suppose the shoulder-blade of an horse to be
long, and in a very oblique direction, so as to
form with the humerus an angle of eighty degrees* ; then, the muscles which move the shoulder forward, backward, upward, and downward,
being remote from the centre or axis of the motion, will produce the flexion and extension of
this part more advantageously than if they were
brought nearer that centre ; so that if the shoulder inclines backward with forty degrees of obliquity, it must advance forty degrees to find the
perpendicular. If, on the contrary, this part,
when in a state of inaction, approaches nearer the
perpendicular, and is in itself naturally, shorter,
the portion of the circle it describes will be less,
whatever may be the intrinsic power of the mus-

D 2   cles.

* See plate iii. fig. 3 & 4.

cles.   The good or bad construction of the shoulder influences materially on progression, since it is the origin of the limb, and consequently its motion determines that of the inferior parts.   It is therefore with good reason that a long and oblique shoulder is required in an horse for speed; since the longer and more oblique that part is, the further the arms of the lever will be extended, the more open will be the angles, and the greater the portion of the circle which it will describe.

To convey an idea of the consequences I am going to draw from the dimensions of Eclipse, I shall endeavour to apply some mechanical principles to the action of the hock, as being that part whose function is of the greatest importance in the progression of the horse.   All horsemen agree in the choice that is to be made in this part; they prefer that one which is wide and flat, because it appears to denote strength; the dissection of the part confirms this opinion.

The

The structure of the hock presents an angular spring, formed by the tibia and the calcaneum*, whose power is increased or diminished in proportion to its shortness. At the union of the two branches of this spring is the origin of the fulcrum, which rests upon the ground. The power which extends these branches is the contraction of the flexor muscles ; the weight of the body is a second power which compresses the spring ; the resistance exists in effect in the extensor muscles, which yield at the moment of flexion, but in their turn re-possess themselves of the power, by which they produce in the spring of the hock an extension equal to the compression it had sustained : for, by the nature of the spring, its extension must be always in the same direction with the compressing power, and with a force equal to the degree of compression. This may be easily perceived in an horse galloping at full speed. In a race-horse, for example, we see the hind legs placed obliquely forward under the body, and

even

* See plate iii. fig. 1 & 2.

even beyond the centre of gravity ; in this direction, finding themselves charged with the whole burthen, they make a sudden effort to disengage themselves from the weight which oppresses them ; and from the repetition of these alternate flexions and extensions proceeds the celerity of the gallop. In horses, on the contrary, whose hind feet do not sufficiently approach the centre of gravity, and whose spring is perpendicularly compressed, we see that the extension still takes place, in the same direction, and in the same proportion. This is distinctly evident in the short gallop of the manage-horse. In a word, the force of action in the hock will increase in proportion with the prolongation of the hinder branch of the spring, formed by the calcaneum ; and we must thence infer, that the wider the hock is, the better it will serve progression ; provided that the remainder of the limb is in just, relative proportion.

This slight idea of the mechanism of the shoulder and the hock will discover the principles upon which I endeavour to establish the advantage of a due proportion of the parts.   It will be readily perceived, that these principles must have for their object the length, breadth, and direction of the solid parts which compose the skeleton of the machine; whose symmetry and harmonious arrangement, favouring the power of the muscles, is the cause of the freedom and extent of the motions.

Though it is not possible to lay bare to our inspection the bony and muscular parts of the living animal, yet the eye, instructed by anatomical knowledge, is able to discern them, and to measure and compare them with sufficient exactness to be able to deduce some consequences concerning the power and the extent of their action.   By this method I took the proportions of Eclipse when living, and have since his death satisfied my curiosity upon his skeleton, having dissected him myself.

It

It is necessary, before I produce the table of the proportions of this famous horse, to apprise the Reader, that I have no intention of establishing the beauty of race-horses by the rule and compass. He must, therefore, banish from his thoughts all idea of a beauty of caprice, or convention, and endeavour to conceive a beauty founded on the natural and mechanical excellence of the animal, and relative to the uses for which he is designed ; namely, in the instance before us, for speed.

The repeated races which Eclipse won, without ever having been beat, prove evidently the superiority of his speed over that of the horses which run against him. It is on this account that I have made choice of him, for a rule to guide me in the reflections which I propose to offer in the course of this essay.

Table

ADVERTISEMENT.

THE want of principles in the veterinary art, as also of some scientific work upon that subject, had made me resolve to publish the Elements of Comparative Anatomy, to serve as a foundation for the studies of the veterinary school; but being deeply impressed with a sense of the pernicious practice which at present obtains among farriers in the art of shoeing, I thought it my duty to apply myself, first of all, to this important point, on which entirely depends the destruction, or preservation of the foundations of the whole machine. With this view, I determined to publish my New Principles of the Horse-Shoe. I shall observe, that if any should apprehend that I have brought this new system from France, they are mistaken; and I believe it to be impossible to produce an instance of any country, in which the shoe I recommend for preserving the foot has been used; or of any author who has even described it. In support of what I advance, I have given a brass shoe, representing that employed in the veterinary schools of France (See Shoe No. 5). It may

be

be said, that my method of paring the hoof is not new, and that it has been described by other writers; this I do not deny, but I have carried farther than them the consequences I have drawn from the same principles. It may be also said, that I am not the first who has given an anatomical description of the foot. To this I do not pretend, nor is it possible to avoid repeating what others have said before me. Hence, then, there will be found an entire agreement between the fundamental principles I have laid down, and those in the little work of the Earl of Pembroke; which, to use a common expression, contains almost as much matter as words; as also those of the excellent treatise of Mr. Clark, which bears so great a resemblance to that last mentioned in what regards the art of shoeing, that they seem qualified to form but one volume. The accordance will be found as great with the principles of M. La Fosse, and of M. Bourgelat, to whom, in many particulars, I owe the tribute of just praise.

I am well aware, that my work will not escape the eye of criticism; and whenever such criticism shall be well founded, I shall receive its correction with thankfulness. But when it shall appear to be only a morose, or common-place censure, I shall observe a perfect silence, and repel it with profound contempt.

I have long foreseen the innumerable difficulties which accumulate before me; and I cannot say they surprize me. I feel myself, however, sufficiently bold to encounter them. The task which

my

my present situation imposes on me is great, but I shall exert every ability to fulfil it; and if the society, which now honours me with its confidence, shall continue for any length of time to do so, I shall make every effort to correspond with their candour, by rendering myself useful in my station.

N.B. I have inserted no anatomical plates in this work, because I consider them to be entirely inadequate to the purpose of instructing; and because I am convinced, that actual dissection alone can enable a student to obtain a proper knowledge of anatomy.

PRELIMINARY DISCOURSE.

THE branch of science which I have the honour to profess in this school, is altogether new in this country, and the name by which it is called, is but little known; it becomes indispensable, therefore, to communicate, for the information of the students, whatever may be learned upon that head.

Veterinary is a word derived from the Latin *veterinarius*; a term appropriated to express, either that part of medicine which regards the cure of morbid animals, or the persons who practice that cure. Several learned men have attempted to discover the origin

origin of the word, which, nevertheless, appears involved in great obscurity. Some have derived the word *veterinus* (from whence *veterinarius* has been formed) from vecto, to carry; "quasi animalia ad *vecturam* idonea;" or from *veho*; " veluti *vecterina*, vel *veheterina*." Others have deduced it from *venter*, the belly; because beasts of burthen carry their loads attached to their belly; " quod onus ad *ventrem* religatum gerit." They who wish to examine these learned attempts, may consult Gesner's edition of R. Stephen's Thesaurus; Fabricii biblioth. Latin.l. 3, c. 12, not.; and the note to Lucretius, lib. 5, l. 863, in Havercamp's edition. What the true etymon of the word may be, is a question of some phylological intricacy, though but of little importance; it is sufficient here to say, that the word *veterinarius*, as used by Columella and Vegetius, signifies a practitioner in one particular part of medicine, namely that which respects the cure of diseased cattle; and that *ars veterinaria*, signifies the art of healing, applied to the healing of cattle.

The

The word *hippiatric*, is a compound term, formed of the Greek word, *hippos*, a horse; and *iatrice*, medicine. This word, therefore, expresses that part of medicine which treats of the cure of diseased horses in particular, and constitutes a principal branch of that division of medicine, which treats of the diseases incident to cattle in general, and to all other domestic animals.

We have undoubted evidence, that this art was cultivated in very early times. In the infancy of medicine, when the art of healing was confined to the rude elements of surgery, it was indiscriminately applied to the relief of all accidental distresses to which the animal frame was liable; whether they occured in man, or in those animals which constituted his wealth, or were the associates of his labours. In these times, many things concurred to attach the minds of men to the well-being of their cattle. They were almost solely used for tillage, and the dairy; and the life and health of the herds was an especial concern. It was forbid by an ancient law in Greece,

under

under pain of severe penalties, to kill a labouring ox[*]. Cattle was the great medium of exchange, before the invention of coin [†]; and the riches of countries and individuals were estimated by the quantity of their cattle; whence we may reasonably infer a proportionate attention to their condition and preservation. And the laws of religion, which rigorously forbad the sacrificing of any animal, but such as were in the most perfect state of health and form[‡], confirmed the necessity of giving due attention to that object.

Chiron the Thessalian, a personage whom antiquity held in extreme veneration, and who, from his transcendant skill in horsemanship, and many other useful arts, was called the wise Centaur, lived to the age of the Trojan war. This great man descends to us as the father of medicine, and the instructor

---

[*] Ælian. Var. Hift. lib. 5. De Animal, lib. 12. Varro de re Rufticâ, lib. 2. Plin. lib. 8, cap. 45.

[†] Columella, lib. 6. Prœm.—Smith's Wealth of Nations, vol. 1, p. 34.

[‡] Archæologia Græca, Potter. lib. 2, c. 4.

of

of Æsculapius in that art. He was, on the concurrent testimony of antiquity*, profoundly skilled therein, as also in the care and management of cattle†; and although we may not affirm, that the treatise on the hippiatric art, which Suidas informs us was current among the antients under his name, was really his production, yet we may fairly infer, from their belief of it, their opinions of the importance and antiquity of that art, and of its intimate connection with general medicine. We meet in Xenophon with proof, that it had been cultivated before his time; in his treatise on horsemanship he cites Simon, an Athenian, who makes mention of Micon, who had applied himself to the study of this branch of medicine. Before the fate of Carthage, Mago had carried this, as well as every other branch of rural science so far, that Columella does not scruple to call him the father of Roman agriculture‡; his works were afterwards translated from the Punic

* Alb. Fabricius. vol. 13.
† Columella, lib. 1. Proem.
‡ Columella, lib. 1. c. 1. Plin. Nat. Hist.

tongue

tongue by order of the Roman Senate. What remains of the antient writers upon this subject, are to be found among the *Scriptores Rei Rusticæ*, published by Gasper; among the Greek collection entitled *Geoponica*, of which the edition of Niclas, printed lately at Leipsic, is the best, and among the *Hippiatrice*, published by J. Ruelle, at Paris, in 1537. These contain all that is preserved of Vegetius, Apsyrtus, Hierocles, and the most celebrated of the old veterinarians.

It would be to no purpose to trace the progress of this art minutely through all its vicissitudes; it is sufficient to say, that the decline of the Roman empire, and the decay of arts and science, occasioned for a time the destruction of this, as well as every other branch of knowledge. But, while veterinary medicine was lost in the west; and was declining fast in Greece, it found an asylum among the Arabians; a nation destined, it should seem, by providence to receive in trust the knowledge of Europe, until, emerged from the abject state into which it was

plunged,

plunged, it was able to reassume its intellectual rank. This nation, which, among other parts of science, cultivated medicine with uncommon ardour, did not neglect this particular part of it, of which we are at present discoursing. This curious fact has entirely escaped M. M. Vitet and Amoreux, in their investigation of the writers on this subject. Herbelot, in his *Bibliotheque Orientale*, informs us, that there are many works on this subject in Arabic*, some of which are in the royal library at Paris.   In the twelfth century, a period at which Arabian learning, especially medicine, was at its height, the Moors of Spain boasted Ibnu, *El Baitar* or *the Veterinarian*, a native of Malaga.   This learned physician and botanist is spoken of as one of the great ornaments of his country, and of the age in which he lived.   He travelled over Africa, Persia, and India, for the improvement of botany, in which excursion he added above two thousand new plants to the herbal of Dioscorides; he afterwards exercised his own profession in the service of the

* Herbelot. Biblioth. Orient. in Verb. *Beithar*—

Sultan

Sultan Saladin, and died at his native Malaga in A. D. 1216[*]. He has left behind him a large treatise on the virtue of herbs; on poisons; on metals; and on animals; the whole reduced into alphabetical order, in three volumes. He is not the only learned Arab who has added to his name the quality of El Baitar, or Beitar, i.e. Veterinarius; from whence the Spaniards have borrowed the term of *Albeytar*, to signify the same thing; as from *El Beitarah*, they have formed *Albeyteria*, to signify, mulomedicina, or the veterinary art. Herbelot mentions also, Abubecre al Beithar, master of the horse to the Sultan Mohammed Ben Calann, who began to reign in Egypt, A. D. 1279, of the Hegira, 678[†]. He is author of a work on the medicine of horses, and on the art of breaking them, which is to be found in the royal library at Paris, marked No. 940, *Kamel al Sanatrin*[‡]. It is worthy of remark, that the Asiatics appear to have preserved that part of the manage-

---

[*] Biblioth. Arabico Hifpan. tom. 1. Carter's Journey from Gibralter to Malag. v. 2. p. 239.

[†] Herbelot. in Verb. *Abubecre* and *Camel*.

[‡] Herbelot. in Verb

ment

ment of horses, which consists in their treatment when diseased, entirely separate from the business of the farrier; the confusion of which essentially distinct occupations, has been hitherto the bane of veterinary science, among us. In the establishment of Akber, the Mogul emperor, who lived in the end of the sixteenth century, we find the distinct office of, *Beitar*, or horse-physician; and *Nalbend*, or farrier[*]; and the Spaniards still distinguish between the Albeytar, and the *Herrador*, or farrier. From the Arabians (for so we may consider the Moors) the Spaniards derived their skill in this art, as well as their valuable breed of horses; which they wisely considered as an object worthy every effort of their medical abilities. And here we may in a few words observe, that if the Spanish writers upon this subject, who are numerous, have not enlarged the boundaries of veterinary science, they have at least this great merit, that they have formed a just opinion of its importance, and have made veterinary medicine keep pace uniformly with the condition of human medicine among them; so that their deficiency in medicine in

[*] Inſtitutes of Akber, tranſlated from the Perſian. v. 1. p. 177, 178.

general, is the real cause of their backwardness in this particular part of it.

It is not improbable, that the taste for science excited by the Arabians, and which as far as respected medicine, laid the foundation of the school of Salerno in Italy, may have been instrumental in rousing the attention of the curious to the veterinary art, but it is not to them that we immediately owe its recovery; especially in that improved state, in which it has began of late to shew itself in Europe.   When learning began to revive, and the activity of genius to be excited for the restoration of science, the medicine of animals, as might be expected, was not an object of principal anxiety.   On the contrary, it still continued in the debased condition in which it had so long subsisted, while the other arts, and among them the art of human medicine, began to make a hasty progress toward science.   Thus neglected, it remained in the hands of those to whom ignorance had consigned it, who being more conversant in horses, were more capable of treating them in a state. These men availed themselves of the opportunity, and partly induced by vanity, partly by interest, openly professed themselves practitioners in this line. They worked on without principles, amassing whatever tradition preserved, encreasing their code of prescriptions by every novelty with which credulity and superstition provided them. Such was the general state of veterinary medicine at home and abroad at the beginning of the sixteenth century, when Francis the first of France gave orders to J. Ruelle, his physician, a canon of Paris, to collect together, from the writings of the antients, whatever might tend to improve this neglected division of the art; which collection was soon after made, and printed at Paris ; first in Latin, in 1530, by the title of *Veterinariæ Medicinæ Scriptores Græci*, in fol. and afterwards in Greek, in 1537. This publication, and the books of Vegetius, which had been lately printed at Basil, began to be read by the learned, and the ardour for perusing the writings of the antients, which in that age strongly prevailed, gave them a value beyond what their intrinsic worth, perhaps, had deserved

served. They, however, began to excite the attention of the curious, among the faculty, and to convince them of the importance of veterinary medicine, properly conducted, to the cause of medicine in general. Hitherto, the system of practical farriery had derived no real service from these acquisitions to the studies of the curious, but it might have been safely predicted, that from the period when men of learning and science deigned to consider its condition, it would, sooner or later, begin to improve. The exertions made for this purpose were, indeed, few; but it was presently perceived, that attention to veterinary science, was of all methods the best calculated to promote comparative anatomy. Accordingly, towards the close of the same century, we find J. Heurnius, otherwise Van Heurn, a learned professor of medicine in the university of Leyden, recommending to his medical students to peruse the writers upon this subject. " Animi causa," says he, " inspicias etiam interdum Geoponicos, et Hippiatros.*"

* De Studio Medicinæ bene inftituendo, Differt.

And

And a few years after Heurnius, the great Lord Bacon, sensible of the service which had been rendered to medicine by zootomy with a view to comparative anatomy, makes the following observation. "In the inquiry which is made by anatomy, it is true which was antiently noted, that the more subtile appear not in anatomies, because they are shut and latent in dead bodies, but open and manifest in life, which being supposed, though the inhumanity of this *anatomia vivorum* was by Celsus justly reprobated, yet in regard of the great use of this observation, the inquiry needed not by him so slightly to have been relinquished altogether, or referred to the casual practices of surgery, but might have been well diverted upon the dissection of beasts alive, which, notwithstanding the dissimilitudes of their parts, may sufficiently satisfy the enquiry*." And in the middle of the following century, Mr. Boyle urges it in still stronger terms, and considers it, both according to its direct object, and its collateral advantages. The diligence

* Advancement of Learning, book 2.

D

of

of zootomists," says he, " may much contribute to
illustrate the doctrine of androtomy, and both inform physicians of the true use of the parts of the
human body, and help to decide divers anatomical
controversies. For, as in general it is scarce possible
to learn the true nature of any creature from the
consideration of the single creature itself; so particularly of divers parts of the human body, it is very
difficult to learn the true use, without consulting
the bodies of other animals, wherein the part in-
quired after is by nature either entirely left out as
needless, or wherein its different bigness, or situation,
or figure, or connection with, and relation to other
parts, may render its use more conspicuous, or at
least more discernable." And further; " It would
be no new thing for naturalists, not professedly physicians, to treat of this subject; the naturalist may
afford good hints to the practitioners of physic, by
trying upon brutes variety of hitherto untried medi-
caments or remedies, and by suggesting to him both
the events of such trials, and also what hath been
already observed about the cure of diseases incident

to

to beasts." And again, " The skilfullest physicians might, without disparagement to their profession, do it an useful piece of service, if they would be pleased to collect, and digest all the approved experiments and practices of farriers, graziers, butchers and the like, which the antients did not despise, but honoured with the titles of *hippiatrica* and *veterinaria*; and among which, if I had leisure, divers things may be taken notice of, which might serve to illustrate the *methodus medendi*." These are a few of the sentiments of ingenious men, selected of many; but they are sufficient to prove, that from the period at which veterinary medicine first attracted the notice of the learned, it grew more and more an object of their attention. I shall follow the progress of this opinion no farther, but shall observe, that after a course of many years, the government of France undertook to give effectual assistance and protection to this most useful part of domestic science, and to provide for it the same advantages by which medicine had been formerly advanced.

* Boyle, vol. 2. p. 169. 4to.

D 2

It

It will not be out of place to give here some account of the means which the French government employed in order to bring about the desireable end; which justly entitles France to the same honours, with respect to the veterinary art, which the world must ever concede to the school of Salerno with respect to medicine; namely, of having first reduced the principles of that art to a foundation of regular science. On the 5th of August, 1761, the council of state issued a decree, empowering Mr. Bourgelat to establish in the city of Lyons a school, in which might be taught the knowledge and treatment of diseases incident to cattle of every description. M. Bourgelat published, without loss of time, a plan of the new establishment, which was well received by the public, and spoken of in the best journals with the greatest applause.

Sensible of the advantage that must result from such an institution, government granted the sum of 50,000 livres, or about 2083l, sterling, payable in six years, at the annual rate of 8333 livres, to defray the

expences

expences of house-rent; providing a laboratory, dispensary, physic garden; stables to serve as hospitals; forges, instruments,and utensils; also rooms for study and dissection; in a word, every thing that might serve to render thc establishment complete. The smallness of the sum granted will appear the less extraordinary, when it is known, that it had been always intended to. apply the produce arising from the hospitals, forges, and dispensary, entirely to the support of the school.

The first school was opened on the 1st of January 1762; it was very soon stocked with native students, and a short time after the numbers were increased by foreigners, among whom were several supported by the Empress Queen, the kings of Denmark, Sweden, Prussia and Sardinia, and the different Swiss cantons. The institution gave early proofs of its utility, in the signal services it rendered to the inhabitants of the country, by affording, on frequent occasions very effectual assistance in cases of epizootic or contagious distempers, and many other particular

cular diseases, to which the brute creation, especially in a state of domesticity, are unfortunately too subject. This determined the king to grant by a decree of the 31st of June, 1764, a special mark of his satisfaction, by permitting it to assume the title of royal veterinary school. At the same time, his majesty conferred on M. Bourgelat the brevet of director and inspector general of the royal veterinary school of Lyons, and of all other similar schools to be hereafter established in the kingdom ; and having given orders that several other schools should be formed upon the same plan as that at Lyons, and especially one in the neighbourhood of the capital, the castle appeared, by its situation and extent, and by the conveniences which the different structures already erected offered, the most eligible place for the second projected establishment.

This building was obtained by purchase in Dec. 1765. M. Bourgelat immediately invited some of the students from Lyons, who had made the greatest progress in the art, placed them for the winter in
Paris,

Paris, and employed them in dissecting and making anatomical preparations of various kinds, which at the opening of the school, served as proofs of the abilities of the pupils he had trained up. In the mean while apartments were building at the new school, capable of receiving 90 students, with dissecting room, laboratory, physic garden, &c. and hospitals able to contain 100 animals, affected with various diseases; the whole of which was completed in October following. Since that time, a riding-house has been added, that nothing might be omitted, which could contribute to the better instruction of the pupils; and the place has been adorned with a variety of curious and useful animals from different parts; such as rams and goats, from Spain, India, the Cape, Barbary, and Angola; cows from different countries, &c. by which the students are furnished with an opportunity, not only of knowing the greater parts of the diseases incident to these different animals, but also of making experiments and observations capable of extending veterinary knowledge. For the same purpose,

purpose, a flock of sheep, and other domestic animals are constantly kept in exhibition.

The interests of rural life were not alone promoted by this establishment, the different corps of cavalry also have repeatedly experienced its benefits. In 1769, each regiment sent a person to be instructed in the school, which persons were quartered in the neighbourhood, and a regulation of the 15th October of the same year provided, that the barracks should be under the direction of a commanding officer, and the studies and interior discipline of the school, should be regulated by the director and inspector general, and by the assistant director. With a view to perpetuate this advantage to the army with less expence, and to provide a constant succession of persons really qualified to serve as farriers in the different regiments, a new regulation of February 1774, confirmed in part that of 1769, but provided, that the military pupils should be reduced to the number of twenty, and lodged in less expensive quarters,

situated

situated neaer to the school, and that no more should be sent from the regiments; and the commanding officer was ordered to engage journeymen farriers to serve in the heavy and light horse, and to present them, preferably to all others, to the director and inspector general; and the same regulation appointed the discipline by which the military pupils were to be governed. With respect to the other students, in order to provide against the obstacles they might encounter in the provinces where they proposed to profess veterinary medicine, a decree was issued, enacting, that all pupils of veterinary schools, who, for the space of four years successively, should have gone through their regular course of study, should be permitted to profess that art in the places where they might fix their residence, or wherever else they might be occasionally called.

The expences attending this school, under the ancient government, including the appointments of the director general, professors, and other officers; ground rents, repairs, and all other contingencies; amounted

E   annually

annually to the sum of 60,000 livres, or 2500l. sterling. These expences were afterwards reduced by the National Assembly.

On the 1st July, 1790, the school at Alford consisted of the following officers.

GOVERNORS.

The Controler General of the finance.
The Intendant of the finance.

DIRECTORS AND PROFESSORS.

Director and Inspector General.
Assistant Director, professor of anatomy and operations.
Professor of materia medica, having the care of the dispensary.
Professor of the exterior knowledge of animals, &c,
Professor, charged with the care of the hospitals.
Professor, having the care of the forges.
A Chaplain and Surgeon.
A Commanding Officer, with his corps.
A Commandant in second------A Commissary.

A report was made in the National Assembly by their committee of finance, of the state of the veterinary schools, and it appeared in the printed account, that the annual expence of these schools amounted together to the sum of 72,000 livres, or 3000l. sterling.

In the following detail, the school of Lyons is not included. From the year 1765 to 1782, the annual expence of Paris school amounted to the sum of 60,000 livres. From 1782 to August 1787, the expences exceeded all bounds, and a debt was contracted exceeding 300,000 livres. Since the year 1787, the ordinary expences were fixed at 42,000 livres, or nearly 1350l. sterling. It must be observed, that a farm which cost 200,000 livres, or above 8000l. sterling, was annexed to the school, the produce of which it entirely consumes. It was proposed to the committee to transfer the school to Paris, but the proposal was rejected, because the pupils met with fewer avocations, and less interruption from their studies in their present situation;

E 2   and

and because the academical appearance of the place had a tendency to ennoble the studies, and to elevate the minds of the young people. The only object now was to fix the expences, and the following establishment was decreed.

	livres.
A Director at - - - - - -	11,000
A Coadjutor performing the functions of professor of anatomy	5,000
Three other professors, each at	2,000
A porter - - - - - - -	300
Anatomical expences - - -	1,200
Expences attending the museum	600
Forges - - - - - - -	1,200
Expences for printing - -	400
For reparations of the building	3,000

£.   s.

Total   28,000 or 1,166 16

Besides the foreign students supported by the crowned heads above mentioned, there were several from

from different countries, who studied in these schools on their own private account. " From every country in Europe," says Mr. Arthur Young, " except England; a strange exception, considering how grossly ignorant our farriers are, and that the whole expences of supporting a young man here, does not exceed 40 livres a year; nor more than four years necessary for his complete instruction."[*]

But those princes were not satisfied with sending pupils to study in France, they presently thought of providing similar institutions at home; and, accordingly, one was soon afterwards established at Vienna; another in Denmark; others in Sweden, Prussia, and Piedmont; and one also, by his present majesty, in the electorate of Hanover. We may now add, that England is at length in possession of an establishment of the same nature; and one that, while it does that honour to the nation, which most of its public institutions confer, from being the work of individual ex-

[*] Travels in France. p. 67.

ertions,

ertions, supported by general opulence and discernment, appears likely, from its particular constitution, to render especial services to the art it protects. Two things, however, it will be essentially necessary to attend to, in the infant state of the institution; the one, to give a free and unembarrassed scope of acting to those who are charged with the arduous task of preparing the elements of a new science, and resisting the force of inveterate prejudice; the other, to exclude from the tuition of the youth, all persons partially, and not fundamentally, versed in the science; such as have a confined, and general acquaintance only, either with farriery or surgery: for otherwise, the stream will be immediately obstructed in its course, the fountain-head of the science will be disturbed and obscured; and those very errors and systems, which ought by every method to be excluded from the school, will be interwoven with its first and fundamental principles.

It remains for me now to give the reader, unconnected with the college, some account of myself, and

and of the situation which I have the honor to hold in this country.

Being superseded in a promotion which I had a right to expect, through the then master of the horse to the king of France, I resolved to come over to England, and to pass some time in observing the state of rural economy in this country, in examining the different breeds of cattle, and especially horses ; in a word, whatever had any relation to the principal objects of my favourite profession. I communicated my design to M. Broussonet, M. D. perpetual secretary to the Royal Society of Agriculture in Paris, and fellow of the Royal Society of London. His reply to me was remarkable. He told me, that if I went to England with the above intentions, I should be astonished at the beauty and value of the domestic animals of all kinds, and that I should find agriculture in the highest state of perfection; but that I should find the veterinary art totally neglected. But, he added, that if I were inclined to risk some proposals for improving that art, he would almost un-

dertake

take to answer for their being well received. He gave me letters of recommendation to Sir Joseph Banks, Bart. and to Dr. Simmons. Thus encouraged, I came to England, in June, 1788. Two months after my arrival in London, I published proposals for forming a veterinary school, but they produced no effect. This disappointment, however, did not destroy my hopes, for in the month of October, 1789, I published fresh proposals, to read lectures on the veterinary art. These proposals met with no better success, and I confess this second disappointment nearly disheartened me. I endeavoured to trace the secret causes which so stubbornly resisted my success, and I soon perceived, that the opulence and mild government of England offered an endless field to foreign adventurers of every description, by whom the nation was daily imposed upon; and that repeated experience of such impositions must naturally excite mistrust towards foreigners in general; and as the honesty of my views was not written on my face, patience and perseverance became my only resource.

About

About this time I had the good fortune to become acquainted with a gentleman, who was led, by a decided taste for the art, and a long desire of seeing it introduced into his own country, to engage in frequent discussions with me on the subject; I made him acquainted with the whole of my plans, and of the little encouragement I had met with. This gentleman eagerly corresponded to my views, and bid me not despair of success, assuring me, that by persisting in my proposals, the reason of the thing would, sooner or later, carry the victory. He had also the friendship to give me particular assistance in drawing up proposals, better adapted to the customs and genius of the nation, which represented, in an able manner, the advantage of studying the veterinary art; these proposals were distributed in May 1790, and consisted of 28 pages in octavo, entitled ; " Plan for establishing an institution to cultivate and teach veterinary medicine."* I carried several of them to Newmarket, where they were well received, and I brought back the names of a few subscribers.

* See Dr. Simmon's Journal.

F

About

About the end of May, I sent several copies to the societies at Odiham, Bath, and Manchester. The former society had, some time before, proposed to send two pupils annually to study in the schools of France, and had opened a fund for the improvement of farriery. On the receipt of my plan, they did me the honour to pass a resolution of approbation, and to elect me an honorary member of their society, and they expressed their opinion of the expediency of establishing an institution similar to those in France, Germany, &c. I added a few names to my subscribers, and deferred taking any further step till the following winter. During this interval, the Odiham society proposed a premium for the best treatise on the glanders, and appointed a committee to meet at the Blenheim coffee-house, to consider of the best method of improving farriery.

This committee met in the close of the year 1790, two treatises only were presented, one by their zealous and respectable vice-precident, the late Sir William Fordyce, and the other by myself. Several
meetings

meetings took place, without any thing very effectual being done, till at length, in one of these meetings, the committee passed a resolution to the following purpose. That they had observed the good effect produced on the public mind by the exertions of the Odiham society for the improvement of farriery, and by my plan proposed, for establishing a public institution for that purpose; that the object of that society was one and the same with that contained in my plan; and that the two schemes ought to be consolidated into one. This was done, and I was appointed professor. A few days after, the committee, by another resolution, detached themselves entirely from the Odiham society; and erected themselves into an independent society (assigning the reasons for taking that step) by the name of, the Veterinary College, London.

This is a simple and fair statement of the case, and of the origin of the Veterinary College; as the gentlemen who uniformly attended, and the official books of the society, can fully evidence. I shall now,

before

before I close this discourse, produce, in proof of what has been above advanced, a few examples of the benefits which mankind at different times have derived, both in the enlargement of their anatomical knowledge, and the improvement of the method of healing, from an inspection into the structure of different animals, and from experiments made upon them in a morbid state.

We know that the physicians of all ages applied themselves to the dissection of animals, and that it was almost entirely by analogy, that those of Greece and Rome judged of the structure of the human body. We are told, indeed, that Herophilus and Erasistratus studied anatomy on the human frame, some centuries before the Christian æra, and that the former even dissected living subjects, having obtained the bodies of malefactors for that purpose; but it does not appear that this practice was continued. On the other hand, it is abundantly proved from history, that the great progress of anatomy, till within a very few centuries, was made by the dissection of brutes.

brutes. In Egypt and the east, as also in Greece and Rome, the dissection of the human body was held in abhorrence; nor could any one dare to attempt it, without offending against the authority of the law, or the more formidable authority of public opinion. This superstitious reverence for the dead, which prevailed for many centuries, confined both the Greeks and Arabians to the dissection of apes, and quadrupeds.* Galen has given us the anatomy of the ape, for that of man: and it is clear that his dissections were restricted to brutes, when he says, that if very learned physicians have been guilty of gross errors, it was, because they neglected to dissect animals. The dissection of the human frame was accounted sacrilegious in the time of Francis the first of France; and the Emperor Charles the fifth proposed the question to the theologians of Salamanca,† whether it was lawful to open a human body, in order to become acquainted with its structure. " Which is the less to be wondered at," says

---

* Gibbon, Decline of Rom. Emp. ch. 52.
Coutumes des Peuples, par M. Démeunier, tom. 3. p. 255.

Mr.

Mr. Boyle, " because, even in this our age, that great people the Moscovites have denied physicians the use of anatomy and skeletons ; the former as an inhuman thing; the latter as fit for little but witchcraft." And he mentions one Quirin, an excellent German surgeon, who being found with a skeleton in Muscovy, hardly escaped with his life ; and his skeleton which he was obliged to leave behind him, was burned.* During these superstitious times, however, the foundation of anatomical knowledge was laid; and if we are to regret those prejudices which so long opposed that perfection of the science to which it has since attained, we are no less to admire the compass of anatomical knowledge which zootomy, and the study of the organization of brutes, was able to afford. The same Mr. Boyle, having occasion to mention the scruples we have been speaking of, observes; " It was perhaps on some such account that Aristotle said, that the external parts of the body were best known in man, the internal in beasts." It

* Boyle. v. 2. p. 68. Ufefulnefs of Nat. Philofophy.

would

would be no difficult task to give a regular chronological account of the progress of comparative anatomy, and of the anatomists who applied themselves to that study, but as I do not pretend to write here the history of that science, I shall at present confine myself to the names of a few principal persons, and of the discoveries they made by means of zootomy.

Erasistratus was the first who observed the lacteal veins in kids, which he opened a short time after they had sucked; he observed the valves of the heart; and demonstrated, contrary to the opinion of Plato, that there was, behind the tracheal artery, or windpipe, a canal or passage, viz. the æsophagus, whose office was to convey food into the stomach. Rufus of Ephesus, we are told, described those two parts, the discovery of which is attributed to Fallopius, and from him are called the *Fallopian tubes*, in the second century; these he discovered in dissecting the womb of an ewe, and adds, " That he strongly suspects them to be seminal vessels, and of the same nature with those

those in males, called the *varicous parastate.*"* Galen demonstrated at Rome on living animals, the organs of sound, and respiration, he made several observations on the brain of animals, he also shewed the nerve *recurrens*, and the effect produced by the ligature of that nerve. Vesalius shewed, by experiments on animals, that it was possible to restore suspended animation, by blowing warm air into the trachean artery; which discovery has saved the lives of many individuals. Croon and Hook, two English physicians, repeated the same experiments a century afterwards, and always with success. Wharton, a physician of London, discovered the salivary glands in an ox, in 1659. Eustachius was the first who found out the thoracic duct in the horse, and an hundred years after, the same canal was discovered in man. The immortal Harvey, assisted by experiments made on living animals, effected a total revolution in medicine, by the famous discovery of the circulation of the blood. Dr. Wren, professor in the university of

* Dutens Enquiry, &c. p. 223.

Oxford,

Oxford, made several experiments on living animals, to be assured of the effects of different substances on the blood and solid parts, the result of which experiments was, to confirm the discovery of Harvey, which for the space of forty years, was strenuously opposed.

Gaspar Aselius, professor of anatomy at Pavia, repeated the discovery of the lacteal veins in the messentary, in brute bodies, which had formerly been known to Erasistratus and Herophilus. Pecquet traced them in the thorax, and completed his discovery by that of the thoracic duct in 1647. It was in the bodies of brutes, also, that Bartholinus discovered the *vasa lymphatica*. Stenon, a native of Copenhagen, but afterwards physician to Ferdinand the second, grand duke of Tuscany, discovered in 1661 the excretory ducts of the lacrymal gland in the eye of a sheep. Malpighi, and Bellini in 1765 described the organs of taste and speech, from the dissections of quadrupeds; but here, analogy led them into some errors. Malpighi's observations on the organ of

G ·feeling,

feeling, were first made on the skins of brutes, and afterwards verified on the human skin.   Weiff made experiments on the hearts of living animals, to prove that the auricles were equal.   In 1641, Maurice Hoffman, professor of physic at Altdroff, discovered the excretory duct of the pancreas in a turkey-cock. The peristaltic motion of the intestines was first dis-covered in animals.   In a word, the greater part of the functions of the human frame were first made known by the general analogy subsisting between the functions of animal organization.   I shall forbear speaking of repeated experiments which have been made on these same animals, with a view to explain those phœnomena, the causes of which nature seems to have entirely removed from our comprehension, such as the mystery of muscular motion, of genera-tion, and of the real functions of the brain, &c.   All these fruitless endeavours have given rise to systems, which proved infinitely more prejudicial than useful to the science they pretended to illustrate.   With regard to the advantages which have resulted to the healing art, from observations or experiments made

on

on the bodies of diseased brutes, it would be unseasonable in this place to enter into a prolix account, which would extend too far the limits of this discourse. It is well known that the first purgative medicine was hellebore, which is said in ancient history to have been discovered by Melampus, who observed the effect it produced in his goats. Many such accidental observations, as well as curious experiments, have improved the means of healing. I shall close this account with the testimony of the learned Dr. Freind, who, speaking of the use of the seton, which was in vogue in the twelfth and thirteenth centuries, both in the east and Europe, concludes thus. " I the rather mention this, because it seems to be not improbable that this hint, as many others have been, was at first taken from a practice very common among cattle-doctors. Columella, who wrote in Claudius's time, describes the operation very fully and elegantly, in these words. *Præsens etiam remedium, &c.* The method here used is still in vogue with the herdsmen; and what is proposed by Columella, is with regard to the plague, or some

epidemical

epidemical infection among cows; and accordingly we find, that the same remedy by issues was afterwards applied to a human body in the same distemper; first by J. Arculanus, who flourished in the fifteenth century; and from his example, several physicians in the succeeding age, recommended them as one of the most effectual preservatives in that terrible case."*

From all that has been said, though in a summary manner, it appears, that the science we are here to cultivate, is able in itself, and has given unequivocal proofs of its ability, to enlarge the boundaries of general medicine. It is to be considered, however, at present, but in an infant state; and it is our duty to secure ourselves against the contagion of system and hypothesis. To effect this, it will be our constant care to adopt nothing but what shall have been faithfully examined and proved; to demonstrate nothing but what the understandings of the pupils may fully

* Freind's Hift. of Phyfic. v. 1. p. 45.

apprehend;

apprehend; and to adhere rigorously to the elementary principles of the science. The result of which will be, a simple theory, upon which they will one day be able to establish an enlightened practice, supported by observation and experience.

LECTURES

LECTURES

ON THE

ART OF FERRIERY, OR FARRIERY.

LECTURE I.

LECTURES

ON THE

ART OF FERRIERY, OR FARRIERY.*

LECTURE I.

CONTAINING

The External and Internal Defcription of the Foot.

GENTLEMEN,

IT would be a total loss of time, at present, to attempt to trace the art of shoeing to its origin. It is well known that ancient writers have left us no information on this branch

---

* The word *ferriery*, from whence by corruption *farriery* has been formed, signifies strictly, the art of working in iron ; but custom has appropriated it to express that branch of smithery which is employed in forging shoes for horses, oxen, &c. It is derived from the French *ferrare*, which is borrowed from the Latin, *ferrarius*, or what pertains to iron. Thus, *ars ferraria*, signifies the art of working in iron generally, and is by Pliny said to have been first invented by the Cyclops; " Fabricam ferrarium invenere Cyclopes." A concurrence of circumstances have with us attached to the word *farriery* an idea of medical practice, which is totally foreign to the genuine meaning of the word. Janius. Etymol. Anglican. Ferriour.

of the veterinary art ; and, to produce the passages of authors in which they cursorily mention the horse-shoe, only in order to shew that those passages afford us no instruction, would be making a display of a vain and impertinent erudition. Since then, the antients have contributed nothing to our improvements in this particular, and the moderns but very little, we have no other resource than in our own enquiries, by means of which it is our business to endeavour, in the first instance, to obtain a thorough knowledge of the external form, and internal organization of the part which forms the basis of the whole animal machine, and which is known by the general appellation of the foot.

If nature has rendered elastic those organs whose office it is to move parts of themselves immoveable, she has no less wisely given solidity to others, whose duty it is to support the weight of the whole fabric.

The fibres which compose the foot are intimately united together, and form by their assemblage differ-

ent

ent plans, the particular arrangements of which determine the density, form, and use, of the parts which they compose.

Those which descend from the coronet to the lower circumference of the hoof, form what is called the wall, or crust of the foot; others, with the appearance of flattened lamina, or thin plates, lying one above another, compose the sole; and the fibres which constitute the frog follow, in some degree, the direction of that part.

Several anatomists have taken the trouble to create systems in order to explain the origin of the human nail; instead of following their example, let it be our object to exclude from our enquiries every systematical notion, which far from bringing us conviction, would but lead us into obscurity and error. Whereas, by confining ourselves to the exposition of such things only as are obvious to our senses, we shall in all probability avoid the mistakes of those,

H 2   who

who endeavour to pass beyond the limits assigned
by nature to every effort of human investigation.

To form an idea of the different degrees of density
observable in the hoof, we must divide it perpendicularly, from the coronet to the toe.

We shall then perceive, that the internal surface
of the wall, or crust, is lined by a laminated substance, in which blood-vessels branch out *ad infi-
intum.*

These vessels, which probably degenerate into se-
rous and lymphatic vessels, penetrate into the sub-,
stance of the hoof; convey to it the nutritious juice;
and contribute to the formation of an highly irritable
part; commonly called, the quick.

On examining still farther into the substance of the
wall, or crust, we no longer distinguish blood-vessels,
but discover a porous substance, more compact than
the

the former; from whence exudes a moisture, intended, no doubt, to maintain a degree of constant pliancy in the part.

On continuing our examination, we come to a substance absolutely senseless, and, to appearance, dead; more or less hard; and destined to protect the sensible parts within, from the injuries they would otherwise receive from the hard bodies on which the animal is obliged to tread.

By attending to the general laws of the growth and nourishment of the nail we shall perceive that the hoof grows from the top, downwards; and from within, outwardly; and not, as many farriers have supposed, from its lower surface; so that the internal part, pushes forward the middle part, and takes its place; while the latter, in its turn, is converted into the dead and horny substance, which time naturally destroys. This constant destruction and reproduction, is the same in all organized bodies; and it is perhaps the most wonderful operation in nature.

As

As to the shape of the foot, we know that it exhibits the segment of an oval, opened at the back, and nearly round in front.; that it is divided into the toe, or anterior part; the quarters or lateral parts; the heels, or posterior parts; and the sole and frog, or inferior parts.

It requires no great knowledge of horses to be able to judge whether the foot is proportioned to the leg. By observing the shape of a horse, and by comparing the size of the leg with that of the body, we may sufficiently perceive whether the . hoof be too large, or too wide, too long, or too short, too little, or too narrow. The particular disadvantages attending which defects I shall here endeavour to explain.

If the hoof be too large and too wide, it will indeed increase the stability and firmness of the fabric, while in a state of inaction, because in this case, each of the columns and supporters presents a greater extent of surface to the ground; but this partial advantage

grows

grows into an evil when it is applied to a body capable of *translation*＊, and considered in a state of actual motion; because then, the mass and weight of th foot, overburthens the muscles of the extremity, and retards the progress of the animal. Besides, the excessive bulk of the foot is a proof of greater or less relaxation in the texture of those fibres which compose it, in which case, the diameters of the vessels are increased, the porosities are multiplied, and the fluids abound in them in too great quantities; consequently, this kind of foot is soft, tender, and sensible.

On the other hand, too small a foot, by not presenting sufficient surface to the ground, renders the

---

＊ It has been impossible to avoid introducing the words *translation, progression, percussion*. Though these words may, in the opinion of some, appear too scientific for the subject, yet it will be found, that in considering the motions of animals according to the laws of mechanics, and expressing them with the accuracy which those laws demand, it was not possible to employ more familiar terms without degrading the subject, and adding nothing to its perspicuity. For a fuller conviction of the necessity of recurring to these terms, both in order to speak and to be understood with accuracy, the reader may consult the ingenious work of the celebrated Borelli, " *de motu animalium.*"

leg

leg less stable and firm.   In feet of this description, from the too close union and too great tension of the fibres, the vessels destined to conduct the nutritious fluid are contracted and obliterated; whence proceeds that dryness in the part, which renders the horn brittle, and liable to split.   When the foot is too long and narrow, the heels are generally more or less contracted, and the weight of the body is thrown upon them; and the length of the toe acting as an obstacle to the animal in its *progression*, renders it liable frequently to stumble, and even to fall.

Sometimes the heels are very low, as in horses that have flat feet, and the nourishment is entirely carried to the toe at the expence of the other parts; and this fault is increased if the horse is too long jointed in the fetlock, because its immediate effect is, to transfer the point on which the foot should bear, entirely to the heels.

When the foot is too short, the heels are generally raised too high; and this double defect, renders

the

the basis of the extremity too narrow, and throws the fetlock joint too forward, and too near the perpendicular; by which means the horse is rendered too strait on his legs, and is in continual danger of falling.

If the pastern and the coronet are also too short, a fault we express, by saying the horse is too short jointed, the defect we are speaking of becomes very considerable, since the animal is then thrown entirely straight upon his legs,

But it is not sufficient to observe the general defects of the foot, it is necessary also for us to examine separately its several constituent parts, in order that we may be able to discover, whether they mutually and completely support the weight with which they are loaded.

The direction of the exterior surface of the hoof, or crust, should be moderately inclined; the surface itself should be smooth and even, and free from all

I   irregularities

irregularities or wrinkles, which prove that there is some derangement, more or less, in the part under observation.

The thickness of the hoof ought to be proportioned to the bulk of the foot. In the fore feet, it ought always to be thicker at the toe, than at the quarters and heels; in the hind feet, on the contrary, the heels and quarters are generally thicker than the toe.

The quarters should be equal in their height, and be neither very much contracted, nor very open. All farriers know also, that the inward quarter is always weaker than the outward.

The heels occupy the hinder part of the foot. They should be neither very high nor low, nor very thin. When they are very high, they throw the weight of the body forward on the toe, and produce the same effects which have been shewn to result from too short a foot, and too short joints.

When

When, on the contrary, the heals are very low, the frog is in general proportionably too large: and this part being obliged to sustain too large a share of the weight, is often so much bruised and injured as to render the animal lame.

In speaking of too long a foot it appeared, that if the fetlock joint was too long, it produced the same effect, and occasioned the same inconvenience, as if the heels were too low; but here it is of very great importance to distinguish, whether the heels are naturally too low, or have been rendered so by the mismanagement of the farrier; as will be demonstrated in the course of these lectures.

The heels may also be too thin, in which case they are flexible and weak, and sensibly affected by the slightest pressure, which renders the horse lame. Here also it is necessary to examine, whether this thinness is natural, or has been occasioned by an accidental cause.

The

The frog, which is placed between the heels, and of which it is the continuation, has the form of a V.*

Its size should be proportioned to that of the other parts of the foot. Its substance is spungy, and less compact than the sole.

Too large a frog, whose surface descends below the level of the heels, sustains too great a share of the weight of the body; and the constant pressure it endures from the hard substances to which it is exposed, renders it liable to such bruises, as may eventually occasion a total lameness.

---

* The French call this part *la fourchette*, or the *fork*, from its forked appearance; but leaft the reader fhould fufpect that the word *frog* is a corruption of *fork*, to which both the name and form of the part bears a great analogy, it may not be amifs to acquaint him, that this part was called, both among the Greeks and Romans, by a word which fignified a frog; the former calling it βατραχος, the latter, *ranula*. Apfyrtus, defcribing a horfe perfect in all its parts, requires it to have, *a fmall frog*, and a hard hoof. Where the note obferves, "βατραχος dicitur pars in media ungulâ tenerrima." Vegetius calls this part by the name of *ranula*, or little frog.

On

On the other hand, when this part is too small, and does not reach the level of the heels, it does not receive the share of the weight which it is designed to support, and the heels are deprived of a part, which contributes to maintain their natural extension.

The sole is that part which covers the whole inferior surface of the foot, excepting the frog. The form of the sole should be moderately concave; too great a concavity indicates a foot, contracted and dry. A sole that is full, and level with the quarters, denotes a soft and relaxed foot; but it happens in common, that the foot exhibits a hoof, more or less dried, while at the same time the sole is soft, thin, and without consistence. This fault is occasioned by too free an use of the farrier's butress.

We shall be thoroughly convinced of this truth, if we observe, that few horses are foaled with a natural propensity to flat feet, excepting a few, bred in low and marshy lands. The art of farriery, however, is competent to check even this natural disposition, which

which the bad practice of the present day only serves to increase.

The sole sometimes descends below the level of the quarters, and presents a convex surface. This form which is of all others the most defective, is occasioned by some accidental cause.

Of the exterior parts which compose the foot, it remains only to speak of the arches, or binders, which are situated between the heels and the frog. They are formed by the continuation of the fibres of the heels, which turn towards each other; and, advancing to the extremity of the frog, where they meet, form an acute angle; and acting by mutual resistance from within, outwardly oppose the contraction of the heels.

The knowledge of the external parts of the foot, however necessary, is not sufficient to form a skilful farrier. He must investigate beyond the horny case we have just examined, and make himself well acquainted

quainted with the nature, arrangement, and use, of the parts which it contains. This knowledge will not only prove a sure guide to him in shoeing, but will very frequently also lay open to him the secret cause of many a lameness, which reduce ignorant practitioners to a state of irrecoverable perplexity.

The foot is composed of hard and soft parts. We shall begin with the former.

The bone of the foot is placed in the interior part of the hoof. Its substance is spungy, it has the form of a half moon; and presents three different surfaces, and two edges or rims. The upper surface is subdivided into two smaller ones, which receive the coronet bone. The anterior one is round, corresponding to the external form of the toe; which surface is covered with the laminated substance of which I shall speak hereafter.

The under surface is concave and is in part lined by the aponeurosis of the flexor muscle of the foot, and by the fleshy sole.

Two holes are to be observed, through which vessels pass, distributing themselves into the substance of the bone. Besides these, there are a multitude of porosities dispersed throughout the whole extent of the surface.

The edges are two in number; the upper one corresponding with the coronet, and presenting three eminences ; in the middle, and on each side. To the first, the extensor-muscles of the foot are attached. The other two terminate laterally the edge just mentioned. The lower and sharp edge corresponds to the outline of the toe. The articular bone, which is called by some, the shuttle bone, on account of its resemblance to a weaver's shuttle, is situated at the inferior or lower part of the articulation of the coronet, and the bone of the foot. It presents two small surfaces, which form an articulation with the bone of the coronet. The irregularities observable on the other parts of the surface, give occasion to the insertion of the ligaments.

Over

Over the two upper extremities of the bone of the foot are two cartilages, which extend from the insertion of the tendon of the extensor muscle of the foot, to the hinder part of the heels. Their shape is nearly semi-lunar, and they adhere strongly to the bone on which they tie. They are perforated by several holes, which serve as a passage to vessels. These cartilages are sometimes ossified in old horses.

We give the name of laminated substance, to a multitude of membraneous plates, which are pretty strong, lining on the one part the internal surface of the wall or crust, of which they are an appendage; and covering on the other part, the whole anterior surface of the bone of the foot. These lamina being double, interweave with one another, so as to establish a perfect union between the hoof and that bone.

The fleshy sole, covers part of the inferior surface of the bone of the foot; and is itself covered by the horny sole. It adheres at its circumference to the laminated substance by means of fibres and vessels

K   sels

sels. The hinder part of the surface of the bone of the foot is covered by the aponeurosis of the flexor muscles, in the substance of which it is strongly implanted; and the aponeurosis is in its turn covered by the fleshy frog.

This part is composed of a soft and spungy substance, of the same shape as the horny frog.

The vessels which are distributed in the internal part of the foot, are the arteries, veins, nerves, and lymphatic vessels; to which we may add, the secreting and excreting vessels, distributed round the articulation.

The artery of the leg, or shank, after dividing itself into two branches behind the pastern, penetrates on each side into the interior of the foot, and these branches are distributed through all its parts. The veins follow the same course as the arteries.

Two branches of the nerve distribute themselves equally on both sides. The lymphatic vessels are not

very perceptible. The glands lie between the articulation and cartilages.

This concise description of the several parts of the
foot, is sufficient to enable a person to distinguish
himself in the art of farriery, properly so called; too
minute a detail, in these elementary instructions,
would be productive of great perplexity. We shall
now proceed to take a review of the use of the parts
of which we have been speaking, beginning with the
external.

The wall, the sole, and the frog, form together a
horny box. The wall, from its direction and consistence, is evidently designed to support the greatest
part of the weight of the body; and it is for every
part of its lower circumference, that the point of
rest on the ground is intended to take place.

In a state of inaction, the heels more directly support that weight in proportion to the obliquity of the
line, from the fetlock to the ground.

In

In *progression*, on the contrary, or while the animal is advancing, the toe more particularly receives the weight at the moment of *percussion*, or when the animal presses on the ground, in order to advance its body.

The weight, however, bears in more instances upon the heels than on any other point of the circumference of the wall.

The frog, from its situation, bears only a slight part of the general burthen; but its chief use is, to serve as a cushion, or guard, to the tendon of the flexor muscle of the foot, to which it acts as a sort of fulcrum.

The soft, spungy, and elastic substance of the frog, perfectly fulfils the views of nature, in preserving the tendon in question from the impression of hard and compact bodies, communicating to it every effect of reaction.

The

The sole in its natural state, and enjoying all its strength, may without risk receive a slight share of the weight, particularly in that part which adjoins the wall; but its concave form proves, that it was the intention of nature to keep it as distant from the ground as possible, in order to preserve it from too great a pressure, which would infallibly prove hurtful to the fleshy sole; and the more so, as this last lies between it, and the bone of the foot; that is to say, between two bodies exceedingly hard.

The heels, I have already said, form the two chief points of rest of the foot.

The binders, are a continuation of the fibres of the heels, as has been shewn above; their principal use is, to distend the heels, which, without their opposition, would infallibly contract.

The internal parts of the foot accomplish also particular functions, which are equally reciprocal.

The

The bone of the foot, constitutes the most solid part of the work. It is the basis of the interior mechanism; and receives the whole burthen, which it afterwards distributes to the surrounding parts.

The laminated substance establishes a close connection between the bone of the foot, and the wall; and contributes also to the distribution of the vessels which convey to the whole circumference of the hoof, the nutritious juice necessary for its growth.

The fleshy frog stands in the same relation to the horny frog, which it likewise replaces in its turn.

The arteries convey life to the parts, by means of the blood which they conduct; and the veins take charge of the residue of that blood, which they bring back into the current of circulation.

The nerves distribute sensation.

The

The glands secrete a humour, designed to lubricate the articulated parts, and to prevent by that means, the drying and inflammation, which would otherwise be unavoidably occasioned, by the action and friction to which those parts are exposed.

LECTURE

LECTURE II.

Of the Pofition of the Foot on the Ground, and of the concave Form of the lower Surface of the Foot, confidered in refpect to Shoeing.

HAVING in the preceding lecture described in a concise manner, though sufficiently full for our purpose, the form and organization of the foot, it is our next business to endeavour, by some fixed rule, founded in nature, to determine, what is the best position of the foot upon the ground; which will enable us to form a just idea of the several defects which tend to impair the firmness of the bases of the frame. In order to explain the principles we are about to offer, it is not sufficient to consider the foot alone, we must extend our en-

quiry

quiry and ascend to the very origin of the limb; because it frequently happens, that the faulty position of the foot is the natural consequence of the bad conformation of some other part of the leg.

If we suppose a leg well formed, and the foot on which it is supported duly proportioned, and consider them in a state of inaction, or standing; we shall perceive,

1st. That a perpendicular line, falling from the point of the shoulder to the ground, will touch the hoof exactly at the toe; if the foot were before or behind this line, its position would be evidently faulty.* In many instances, however, as the foot is thrown into one or other of these positions, by the

* The reason of this will appear by considering, firft, that the less the legs of the horse are in the first place intended as columns to support the superstructure; and secondly, that a column then only enjoys its whole strength, when it stands exactly perpendicular to the horizon. Accordingly, in the horse here described, the fore arm and shank bone will be perfectly straight, and parallel to the ideal line falling from the shoulders to the toe.

false

false direction of the leg, we are to take care, in these particular cases, not to attribute to the foot a fault which is not justly imputable to it.

2dly. A perpendicular line falling from the upper part of the knee to the ground, considered in front, will divide the foot into two equal parts in its passage through the center of the coronet to the center of the sole. If this line should fall either on the inward or outward quarter, the foot would evidently be awry. In this case the lateral parts of the foot become unequal either in height or direction, and the toes are turned either outwards or inwards.

The toe may be turned outwards, either by the bad conformation of the foot alone, or by the false direction of some part of the leg. When the fault is in the foot, it proceeds from the inward quarter being too low, in which case the weight of the body pressing more immediately upon it, overburthens it, and prevents its growth; whilst the outward quarter, relieved from bearing a part of the weight which it

ought

ought to have shared, grows and spreads itself at the expence of the other. This fault may be lessened by shoeing, as will be explained in the next lecture. The toe may also be turned outwards by the following defects: 1st. When a horse is narrow-chested, and the elbow being pressed against the ribs, directs the extremity outwards. 2dly. When the knees are turned inwards. 3dly. When the articulation of the fetlock is bent inwards; both of which produce the same effect with the former. In these three cases we may in some degree relieve the inward quarter, but we must not attempt to restore the position of the foot entirely, as advised by a certain author, because in following his advice we should strain the ligaments of the articulations, which no doubt are originally faulty, and to which art can offer no remedy but what is attended with great danger.

The opposite causes to these here described produce the contrary defects: 1st. When the elbow is too much detached from the body, the whole leg, and

and consequently the foot, will be directed inwards. 2dly. When the knees are bent outwards (a deformity which seldom occurs): and, 3dly. when the fetlock is turned outwards. In each of these three cases the art of shoeing can at the utmost only check the progress of the evil, but can never remove it entirely.

There is a cause, not less common, which destroys the natural position of the foot on the ground; namely, when one of the quarters is more forcibly contracted than the other. This contraction is occasioned by the upper surface of the shoe being made concave, which cavity confines the quarters as in a vice;* and also by the practice of cutting away the binders of the sole, and the inner part of the heels. In this state, the quarters being com-

---

. * This will be understood by recollecting, that, action and reaction being equal, when the hoof which is pared away to correspond with the cavity of the shoe, begins to grow within that cavity, the resistance it will there meet with will be the same as if the shoe compressed the hoof, and the effect will be equal.

pressed

pressed by the shoe, and the heels losing that resistance which nature had opposed to their contraction,
draw mutually towards each other; or else, the
weaker yields to the stronger, and the foot becomes
awry.   In these cases, the art of shoeing sometimes
affords a remedy, as will be hereafter explained.

We shall not in this place examine several accidental causes which contribute to vitiate the position
of the foot; such as, false quarters, operations ill
performed, the destruction of the toe and heels, the
too great height of the latter part, as well as the too
great length of the former; these particular circumstances will not authorize us to lay down any general rule in theory, since practice only (as will be
shewn in the practical lecture) can enable us to determine concerning them, and to apply the seasonable relief.

We proceed now to the examination of the inferior surface, or cavity, of the foot, considered in
respect to shoeing.

We

We know that the horse, in his wild state, requires no shoes to protect his feet from the resistance of the ground on which he treads. But, being rendered subservient to the use of man in a domestic state, applied to severe and continued labour, and compelled to tread frequently, and for a long time together, on the irregular and stony surface of the roads, it became necessary to secure his feet from ruin by strengthening them with the iron band which we call, a shoe.

The question, then, is, what ought to be the shape of this shoe; and whether the shoe which is in use at present, is conformable with, or contrary to, the intention of nature.

It is clear to every observing mind, that nothing in nature is the effect of chance; an intelligent principle has evidently presided over the formation of the animated bodies which inhabit this earth, and the same principle has been no less provident in determining the functions of their several parts. In fact,

fact, into whatever part of nature we inspect, we every where discover manifest proofs of a positive design, and of aptness to a particular end. If we examine, for instance, the inferior surface of the feet of all animals, we shall perceive them to be more or less irregular, according to the purposes of their species; that is to say, according to their means of providing themselves subsistence, and of removing themselves more or less speedily from one place to another.

Without adducing instances from the great variety of animated beings with which we are surrounded, and among which the curious observer may hourly find an opportunity to verify this remark, we shall confine ourselves to the examination of the horses foot, which is the proper object of our enquiry. We have already observed, in describing the external parts of the foot, that the sole is always more or less concave; this shape answers two purposes, both of which nature evidently designed in so constructing it. The one purpose is, to make the tread
of

of the foot bear equally on all the points of its circumference; and, at the same time, to raise the sole above the ground in such a manner as to protect it from the violent pressure which would otherwise have unavoidably injured the tender parts contained within the hoof. The other purpose is, to encrease the strength and firmness of the foot upon the ground.*

To

* The irregularity we have mentioned in the lower surface of the feet of all animals, gives rise to several prominences, which enable them to attach themselves firmly to the different surfaces on which they tread, and serve as *fulcra*, or points of rest, adapted to the respective motions of the different species. This we perceive both in the claw, the cloven-foot, and the entire hoof. With respect to the horse, whose nature it is to exert occasionally great strength and great speed upon a surface either flat or moderately inclined, it was necessary he should have a foot with a certain surface, and so constructed as to command a firm footing upon the surface on which he was to tread. Accordingly, nature has given him a vaulted or concave foot, bearing with incredible force upon the lower edge, or foundation of the vault, and capable of maintaining, by means of that cavity, an almost inseparable union with the soil; as this lecture is intended to prove. The antients, to whom the use of the iron shoe was unknown, and who, from not having their ideas perplexed by the different theories of shoeing, valued highly the natural hoof for its obvious utility; directed their attention to the preservation of its natural form, no less than of its consistence. The acute edge, which they cauti-

M ously

To convince ourselves that the cavity of the sole contributes to produce this effect, let us observe a horse treading upon a moderately soft surface, and we shall perceive that at every step the foot leaves in the ground an impression produced by the *ungula* (or sharp edge of the wall) and by the frog; while the sole moulds in bass-relief; so that the lower surface unites itself with the ground, forming a species of articulation, and from this circumstance results a most firm point of bearing, rendering it impossible for the foot to slip or be displaced, while the leg is employed in forwarding the body.

ously retained, was called by the Greeks ονξ, by the Romans ungula.   In the Geoponica the learned editor thus observes of this part. " 'Ονξ cum ab τη οπλη distinguatur, ungulæ debet pars esse anterior inferiorque, cujus firmitas ab antiquis, ferreas soleas ignorantibus, in præcipura ponitur laude." vol. 4. p. 1104.   The same distinction, and from the same cause, seems to have been made by the Roman writers on this subject, between the *unguis* and the *ungula*.   Vegetius recommends, in his first book, to anoint the *ungulæ* after a journey, that by this means, " subcrescat quod itineris attriverat injuria." In the same place he gives directions for cleansing the sole and frog, " soleas ranulasque purgari, quod fortiores *ungulas* reddit."   And a few lines lower he particularly mentions the *ungula* as that part which imprints the ground.   Whereas the *unguis* is considered as the upper surface of the hoof; " coronas vel *ungues* animalium confricabis."

When

When the horse is on very hard ground, the hollow of the foot, it is true, cannot produce an equal effect, but the sharp edge of the wall, and particularly of the toe, will nevertheless fix the foot much more firmly to the ground than if the interior surface was a perfect plane.

These reasons which we have produced here to prove, what were the intentions of nature in thus rendering the lower surface of the horse's foot concave, are so simple and obvious, that it appears unnecessary to adduce examples for their support; in order, however, that we may omit nothing which may tend to convince those who differ from us upon this subject, and who are strongly biassed in favour of their own opinion, we shall offer what appears to us an incontrovertible principle; and should we have the good fortune to succeed in this attempt, we may flatter ourselves with having gained no trivial victory.

The leg of a horse when in action, describes a portion of a circle, proportioned to the length and

M

freedom

freedom of its motions. When the horse advances one of his legs, at the moment the foot touches the ground it describes an oblique line, inclining forward from the shoulder to the ground. In proportion as the body advances, this obliquity is lessened, until at length the leg attains a vertical direction, at which time the horse has completed half his action. All this time the leg has only been employed in bearing the weight of the body; but in continuing the action it begins to project or determine the body forward, which action it continues until it describes another oblique line, equal to the former, but in an opposite direction, inclining forward from the ground to the shoulder, and forming with the first line an angle more or less open; this is the whole extent of the action of the horse, and the foot, firmly fixed on the ground, does not quit its tread till the whole action is completed. This, however, can only be applied to a well formed foot, enjoying every advantage which may result from its structure. Let us now suppose a flat foot, that is to say a foot, the cavity of which is from some cause filled up, or effaced. The

The points of rest on the ground at the moment of progression in such a foot will be far less firm than that of the concave foot, because when the leg, in projecting the body, shall have obtained but a certain degree of obliquity, it will not dare to hazard the whole extent of its action, lest the foot, which has not sufficient hold upon the ground, should slip back. If we carry our thoughts now to the convex foot, it will be easy to conceive that the convex surface of the sole destroys entirely the solid bearing of the foot on the ground; such a foot is constantly in a state of vacillation, and would unavoidably slip back, before the leg could possibly attain its last degree of extension.*

I beg

* This may be reduced to demonstration by comparing the feet of all quadrupeds, which, however they may be diversified or adapted to other particular purposes, agree in one general principle, by which they effect their progression. They are all furnished with a heel, serving as a point of rest while standing, and the opposite side of the foot, or toe, is provided with a sharp angular point, or points, by affixing which to the ground they are able to command any degree of speed. Even man, when running, at each projection of his body inflects his toes to the ground, and by the firmness of that pressure obtains

I beg to observe, that I have employed the extreme points of comparison, in order to render my reasoning the more perspicuous; in further illustration of

tains the last degree of purchase; as may be proved by attempting to run, at the same time keeping the toes from the ground. The cat kind, by means of the excessive sharpness of their claws, which they are able to fix into most substances, so as to ascend a tree and other perpendicular surfaces, are able to secure their footing with proportionate firmness. The dog, whose feet are partly of the same nature, but who is not intended for the same mode of life, is provided with claws less curved and sharp, but which enable him, upon surfaces more inclined, to tread with extreme firmness and tenacity, and by their pressure in the surface of the earth furnish him with a purchase, which enables him to display a surprising speed. The deer, also intended for speed, finds the same benefit in the double angle of his toe, which strikes into the ground, and establishes a most firm tread. The same is to be observed of the horse and zebra, in their natural state; which animals, although they have not an angle visible without, like the others, and though the foot is guarded by a circular defence, yet tread with equal firmness by means of an angular edge. Let us compare in detail the feet of the horse and the dog; and it will appear that they are formed exactly upon the same principles as to progression. The ball of the foot in the dog, corresponds with the heel and frog of the horse, and the five points of the claws, standing in a semi-circle, correspond with the lower edge of the hoof, which may be considered as a succession of points. The former rests on the ball of the foot, as the latter on the heels and frog. In proportion as the body is advanced and the foot retires, the point of rest advances to the toe, in the horse, and to the central claw in the dog.

of these principles, let us consider how much strength is lost by large draft horses, when drawing a heavy carriage up an inclined road. Their feet, which are either flat or convex, slide back at every step before the leg has been able to complete the whole compass of its action. To render this more evident, let us make an arbitrary calculation, and suppose the extent of the possible action of the leg to comprehend 25 degrees;* this it will accomplish, provided the foot can be solidly and firmly fixed on the ground. But if the firmness of the foot is in any degree impaired by its flatness, it will be obliged to quit the ground at the 22d degree,+ and suppose one degree lost by the slipping of the foot backwards, this will

dog. When either animal is stretched to the extent of his limb, the points of the toe and claw are pressed into the ground, and from the purchase there obtained the body is projected. If we were to widen the point of the claw in the dog, by adding to it a small plate of iron, broader than its natural termination, there can be no doubt that the dog would be unable to tread with the same hold, or to extend his limbs to the term of their natural action.

* See pl. 1. fig. F. G.
+ See pl. 1. fig. H. I.

make

make a difference of 4 degrees. But if the inferior surface of the foot is convex, it will quit the ground at the 20th degree;* and if two degrees are added for the slipping backwards, it will make the loss of 7 degrees in the total action of the leg.

With the evidence of the experimental proof before us, let us proceed to lay down a sure and certain principle for farriery, and such as shall enable us to determine the proper shape which the shoe ought to have, when we first apply it to a foot that has never yet been shod.

No one will venture to deny, that whether we consider the inward anatomical construction of the foot, or its outward form; or consider the use of its several component parts, reason directs us to a close imitation of nature. If we apply to the foot of a horse a concave, a flat, or a convex shoe, it is evident that the consequence will be precisely the same as has been shewn to result from feet whose inferior sur-

* See pl. 1. fig. K. L.

face

face are naturally concave, flat, or convex. Suppose, for instance, a foot well formed and properly concave, a second, flat; and a third, convex. The inconveniences attending the convex and flat foot, will be considerably increased by shoes with a similar surface, because the iron of the shoe being harder than the horn of the hoof, presents a smoother and more polished surface, and, consequently, more liable to slip. On this account therefore it is, that we have proposed the concave shoe, that is to say, concave in its lower surface, because it represents the natural shape of the foot, and because it fulfils, in every respect, the views and intentions of nature; and we are therefore convinced that it ought to be applied to all good feet.

As some cases are to be excepted from every general rule, so here the use of the concave shoe is to be excepted from the case of a flat foot, and especially of a convex one; but it does not follow from this exception, that the use of this shoe may not become general in time; because it must be remembered,

N

bered, that feet only become flat and convex through bad shoeing, or by some accident, as when a horse is foundered; and that no horses, not even those bred in marshy and low lands, are foaled with this imperfection. Nor can we be justified in accusing nature with having neglected to provide sufficiently for the foundations of this admirable machine, when at the same time the same machine affords us so many convincing proofs, both of her wisdom, and her providence.

But it is not in the concave form only that the shoe here proposed must differ from the shoe in use among farriers, at this day; there are certain proportions also to be observed in its different parts. Its breadth should be considerably less than the breadth of the common shoe; it is totally unnecessary to cover any part of the sole, especially when care is taken to preserve its natural hardness. The breadth of the shoe at the heels, should be one half of its breadth at the toe. Its thickness should decrease gradually from the toe, so as to be reduced

one

one half at the extremity of the heels. As to the distribution of the stamp-holes, every farrier knows that in shoes for the fore feet they should be at the toe, and quarters, because the wall, or crust, of the fore feet is stronger at the toe than at the heels. The reverse of this is to be observed, in the hind shoes, because the heels, and quarters of the hind feet, are commonly stronger than the toe. It is impossible to lay down any general rule for disposing of these holes in bad feet, it must be the business of the farrier to distribute them in such a manner, as to be able to fix the nails in those parts of the wall where the horn is sound and firm. Farriers generally multiply these stamp-holes too much, which brings the nails too close together, occasions the horn to break in splinters, and at length destroys the wall.

I would recommend the following number for good feet, viz. for race-horses, six; i.e. three on each side: for saddle horses, seven; four on the outside and three within, the quarter on this side being

weaker

weaker than on the other; the same number for coach horses of the middling size; for large coach horses, four on each side; and for cart horses, five on the out, and four on the inside.

It is also of principal importance to determine the weight of the shoe; for it is matter of astonishment to see some horses with shoes weighing each five pounds, making together a burthen of twenty pounds of iron attached to their four feet. It is obvious to common sense, that such an additional weight fixed to the extremity of the leg, must be productive of some inconvenience or other, and in fact the muscles are thereby compelled to greater exertion, the ligaments are stretched, and the articulations continually fatigued; and besides all these evil consequences, the shoe by its weight forces out the nails, and so entirely spoils the texture of the wall, or crust, that it becomes often extremely difficult to fix the shoe to the hoof. Why then, we may ask, do not the practitioners of the present day, who are daily witnesses of these facts, and are indeed the principal authors of them,

them, apply themselves to the correction of their own errors? The answer, I fear, is obvious, because he who is uneducated, and destitute of sound principles in his art, cannot turn to real profit the experience he has acquired, nor abandon the path of prejudice and custom in which he has so long journied; but satisfies himself, with continuing to imitate and repeat whatever he has seen done by others.

The weight which we propose for shoes of different kinds is nearly as follows;

	lb.	oz.
1. For the strongest sort of cart horses,	2	12
2. For the smaller horses of this kind,	1	12
3. For the largest coach horses, - -	1	12
4. For the smaller, ditto, - - - -	1	4
5. For saddle horses of any height 1lb. 2 oz. to 10		
6. For race horses, - - - - 5 oz. to 4		

By reducing the superfluous breadth of these shoes, their thickness may be increased without making any addition to their weight.*

* It will follow that great attention should be paid to the quality of the iron; since the goodness of the metal will allow one to reduce

still

Besides the common shoe for sound feet, there are also others whose various shapes are determined by the necessity of the case, that is to say, by the different derangements and diseases to which the horse's foot is liable. Such, for instance, are, what are called the covered, flat, or convex shoe, the patten shoe, the shoe for all feet, simple, double, and hinged, the shoe without nails, the half moon shoe, the Turkish shoe, the slipper shoe, &c.

The mule being an animal uncommon in this country, the ass of no great value, and the ox not generally employed in labour, we shall dwell but little on the shoeing of these animals. The shoe for the fore feet of the mule is very similar to that which the farriers call, the bar shoe; it is very wide and large, especially at the toe, where it sometimes pro-

still more the size and weight of the shoe. Many persons will no doubt observe, that such light and concave shoes will wear out too soon: I have no objection to agree with them in that respect; but I will ask them, if they would prefer to have their horses lame six months of the year, rather than pay the expence of eighteen or twenty shoes more in the space of twelve months.

jects

jects four inches and upwards beyond the hoof.
This excess is given it with a view to enlarge the
basis of the foot, which is in general exceedingly
narrow in this animal. The shoe for the hind
feet is open at the heels, like the horse's shoe, but it
is lengthened at the toe, like the preceding one.
The former is called in French, *planche*, and the
latter *florentine*.

The ass's foot having the same shape as the
mule's, requires the same kind of shoe, with this
only difference, that the shoe for the fore feet is not
closed at the heels, and that its edges do not project
so much beyond the hoof. It is the same for the
hind feet.

The ox's shoe consists of a flat plate of iron, with
five or six stamp-holes on the outward edge to receive the nails; at the toe is a projection of four or
five inches, which, passing in the cleft of the foot, is
bent over the hoof, so as to keep the shoe in its
place. In many parts of France, where the ox is
used

used for draft, it is sometimes necessary to employ eight shoes, one under each nail; or four, one under each external nail; and sometimes only two, one under the external nail of each fore foot.

I have given this short account, in this place, because it is not my intention to say any thing more in these lectures concerning the shoeing of these animals. .In the next, I shall call your attention to the danger of paring the hoof too much, and to the mischiefs which daily result from the exercise of this destructive method.

LECTURE

LECTURE III.

Of Paring the Hoof, the Accidents resulting from the unskilful Performance of this Operation; and of Shoeing good, flat, and convex Feet.

WHEN a colt is brought to a farrier to be shod for the first time, his first business should be to examine the conformation of the young animal, particularly the direction of his legs; to observe whether the fore legs are perfectly vertical, or whether, on the contrary, they incline backward or forward; whether the pastern is in just proportion, A,* or whether too long, B,† or too short, C,‡ whether the toes are turned inwards, D. D.§ or outwards, E. E‖; he should endeavour, by the principles

---

* See plate the first, fig. A.
† Ditto   ditto   fig. B.
‡ Ditto   ditto   fig. C.
§ Ditto   ditto   fig. D. D.
‖ Ditto   ditto   fig. E. E.

we

we have laid down in the preceding lecture to discover, in which part of the limb the fault exists.

He is then to proceed to examine the foot, and to
ascertain, whether it is proportionate to the leg;
whether its surface is free from defect, whether of a
good consistence; i. e. whether strong or weak, hard
or soft, whether the quarters are equal, the heels
high or low, slender or thick; whether the frog is
in just proportion to the other parts; whether the
sole is strong, or the contrary; and to observe its
degree of concavity.

If the leg and foot are exempt from every defect,
the farrier should begin paring the foot, by merely
cutting off, whatever breaks the level of the inferior
surface of the wall: but he is not to meddle with
the sole, the binder, or the frog. This seems the
proper place to convince him of the necessity of
preserving to these parts their solidity, by laying before him the numberless accidents, attending their
destruction: Let us ask ourselves, what is the drift
of

of the operation of farriery? It is to furnish an additional strength for the foot, to render it capable of resisting the hardest bodies, to which it may be exposed: but, if at the very time we make this addition, we destroy with the butress those parts, which nature has formed with the very same intent, we not only do not increase the resources of the foot, but we destroy that organ, by predisposing it to a multitude of ailments, of which I shall speak hereafter.

By thinning the sole too much, and going beyond the dead horny part, we destroy its organization: for it is not necessary to go so far as to feteh blood, to produce this evil; it is enough only to touch that substance, which receives the glutinous juice through the numberless pores with which the sole abounds. The result is a real wound, which cannot be understood, but by a person acquainted with the laws of the animal œconomy, and of which the mere mechanical practitioner cannot form an idea. " Let us, however, make a comparison, capable of striking the most undiscerning. If, for instance, we take away

from

the upper surface of the bark of a tree, we do it no great injury; nevertheless we rob it of its natural covering; and if we penetrate further into the substance of this bark, we shall produce a real wound; we shall perceive a kind of moisture exuding from the part, which will soon be absorbed by the contact of the air, and drying up the surface of the bark, already too much affected, will produce a scar, more or less irregular, and which will not be effaced, till nature has renewed the bark, an operation, which will require a certain lapse of time.

What should we say of a gardener, who, in order to protect a tree from the fruition of other bodies, to which it might be exposed, should begin to strip it of its bark, with the design of inclosing the body with some artificial covering? we should no doubt look upon him as the most stupid of mortals, yet such a man is the farrier, who destroys the whole external surface of the foot in order to fix on his shoe.

The

The inconveniences that arise from overparing the sole, are not the same in all feet: among those that are hard, narrow, and very concave, as among blood or high bred horses, the drying up of the sole increases the cavity to that degree, that it compresses the fleshy sole, which occasions a constant and a very painful lameness, and which the farrier, who is far from suspecting the true cause, increases every time of shoeing.

When the foot is naturally large and disposed to relaxation, the sole being too much thinned, yields to the afflux of the humours, loses its concavity, becomes flat and even sometimes convex; this accident is very frequent. The sole also, when too much thinned, is liable to be easily bruised by the shoe, stones, or gravel, &c.

It is therefore of the greatest importance to preserve to the sole its natural thickness, and consequently the farrier should only take off with the butress those lamina or scales, which are really dead,

and

and almost detach themselves, especially when they remain too long on old shoes.

I repeat what I have already said, that the frog is intended to bear part of the weight of the body, and that for this reason alone, it ought to be preserved entire. When it appears too bulky as in fat or flat feet, which have generally very low heels, it is better to supply this defect by a slight encrease of thickness in the heels of the shoe, than to strip this part of its horny covering. By this means the heels are raised to a level with the rest of the foot, and the weight is equally distributed to every point of the circumference of the foot.

By cutting the frog to the quick, as is often practised, the part is irritated and inflamed; the humours become abundant, and produce a sharp discharge, which corrodes its own substance, and even that of the heels; and which sometimes in its progress rises to the folds of the pastern, and occasions the disease, which we call the running thrush, a very common affection,

affection, though none would be more rare, if the frog was never pared. Nothing more should be cut away, than those dead and proud parts, which naturally detach themselves by the laws of growth and reproduction.

The heels should be pared according to their strength, height, or depression; and also in proportion to the length or shortness of the pastern, which it is very material to observe; if we remember, that these parts support three quarters of the weight of the whole mass, the necessity of preserving them will be obvious.

The binders, those parts so very essential to the support of the heels, should be preserved with the most scrupulous care : the butress should never touch them, excepting in some very extraordinary cases, when they grow too fast, it then becomes indispensable to cut them level with the heels, but always flat, and never obliquely nor inwards.

To

To judge how very remote the farriery of the present day is from a sound practice, we have only to examine the feet of [horses in general. We shall hardly find any one, whose binders are not destroyed ; nay, more than that, the farrier, by one stroke of the butress, makes a division between those parts and the heels, at the place where the point of bearing lies ; and not satisfied with that, he further separates, with the same tool, the frog from the heel. These two last ruinous operations are the finishing strokes. A farrier, who should be aukward at these, would not be reputed a good workman.

In short, ignorant practitioners, who only see by the eyes of the body, the perception of which is limited to the superficies, operate on a horse's foot, as a carpenter on a piece of wood to polish it.

But how shall we be able to persuade men, unpossessed of the first principles of their art, that their method has hitherto been in direct opposition to the laws of nature ? How make them to comprehend,

that

that instead of opening the heels, they facilitate their contraction? Indeed we shall not attempt it, persuaded we should have to encounter no less obstacles from prejudice, than those which superstition opposed to the demonstrations of Galileo.

It will therefore only be, when veterinary science shall have made a certain progress, and that students enlightened and settled in different parts of the country, have disseminated its principles, that hopes may be entertained of a salutary reform in farriery. But let us here terminate these reflexions, and return to the practice of farriery.

We have already said, that our method of paring a good foot that has never been shod, consisted merely in rendering the wall level, in order to receive an equally level shoe, but that the butress should not be used on any of the other parts.

If it is a good foot that has been shod several times, we are still to take off from the wall nothing

P

more

more than the old horn, which is not sufficiently solid to receive the shoe; and only cleanse the sole and frog from the proud parts, which are ready to come off spontaneously.

When the foot is thus prepared, the concave shoe, No. 1,* is to be applied. Here the old observation naturally recurs, viz. that the shoe should be adapted to the foot, and not the foot to the shoe.

The farrier therefore must pay the greatest attention to make the shoe exactly correspond with the circumference or outline of the foot. This fundamental principle of farriery is generally neglected; of which we may be convinced by casting our eye on figure M, plate 2. which represents the natural form of a colt's foot, compared with figure N, representing a foot ruined by bad shoeing.

Two other causes combine with this in straightening the quarters and contracting the heels, viz.

* See the brass shoe, No. 1.

destroying

destroying the binders and the concave form, given to the upper surface of the shoe, being the very reverse of that which is here given.

The shoe being adjusted to the foot, without pressing the sole, should admit between it and that part just a sufficient interval for the introduction of the pricker, a greater space is liable to admit large gravel or stones, which may bruise the sole, and even occasion sores.

The shoe being nailed on, the farrier should have as little as possible to rasp, and that only from the shoe to the rivets, but never above them, because by rasping the whole surface of the hoof, you not only injure its substance, but you dispose it also to dry. And should the rasp, through the unskilfulness of the farrier's hand, touch ever so slightly the origin of the nail near the coronet, where the part is exceedingly thin, sand-cracks are very apt to ensue, the beginning of which is a small wound or crevice, occasioned by the stroke of the rasp. Hitherto we

have

have been speaking of the shoeing of the fore feet; we shall now enter into some detail respecting the hind feet.

It is no less necessary to examine the direction of the hind legs, and the position of the hind feet, in order to proceed with judgement, in the operation of shoeing. In consequence, the farrier should place himself behind the horse, and trace with his eye, a perpendicular line, which proceeding from the point of the hock, should fall on the sole, passing through the center of the heel. He is to observe, if this perpendicular line falls within the foot, whether the points of the hocks incline to each other; if, on the contrary, it fall on the outward side of the foot, whether both hocks do not incline outwards. In the first case, by viewing the horse in front, he will perceive that the toes of the hind feet are turned outwards; and in the second case, that, on the contrary, these parts are turned inwards. He should then examine the legs sideways, to ascertain whether the hock is too much bent, too straight, or too open.

The

The next step is the examining of the foot, in which is to be considered whether it is proportioned to the leg, whether its shape is natural, its consistence good, and if it is free from cracks. Supposing the leg in a proper direction, and the foot free from natural and accidental defects, he should begin to pare this part also, by taking off from the wall, those pieces of horn only, which breaks the level of the surface, to which the shoe is to be fitted; to clear the sole and frog from all the proud parts, and then make use of the concave shoe. No. 2.*

A flat foot must be pared with great caution; the butress must only touch the wall, in order to divest it of the old horn as much as possible. We must not cut away any thing from the sole or frog, these parts requiring all their strength to resist the humours, which flow to them in too great abundance, whilst the wall, deprived of its nourishment, exhibits itself dried up, irregular and scaly. In this case we are to use the shoe, No. 3.†

* See the brass shoe, No. 2.   † See the brass shoe, No. 3.

The

The convex foot I have already said, in describing the hoof, is that, whose sole extends below the quarters, presenting a surface more or less convex.   This deformity is so much the more dangerous, as the horse is obliged to bear on the ground at the centre of the sole, which would soon render him incapable of service, if not remedied in the shoeing.

A foot may, by a particular habit, be disposed to become flat, the sole may be weak, in a word, the whole texture of the horn may be inclined to relaxation; but nature, we are sure, never deviated so far from her own wise laws, as to intend to give the foot the shape we are speaking of.   This shape is always accidental, and the result of the bad methods of paring the foot to excess, and of giving a concave shape to the upper surface of the shoe.

This last cause, by compressing the quarters, forces down the weakened sole, so as to make it lose its natural shape, and to require a greater or less degree of convexity.

It

It is not in this case only, that this bad shape of the shoe produces dangerous consequences, the strongest feet are impaired by it; it crushes the quarters, and contracts the heels, from whence a compression of the quick parts ensues, and consequently lameness in a great number of horses. There is no method of remedying the convex foot, and we may think ourselves fortunate, if we are sometimes able to check its progress. The manner of paring it is the same as for the flat foot; the sole must be most cautiously pared, and use made of the shoe, No. 4.* the shape of which must be altered relatively to the state of the foot; it is evident, that there is no possibility of establishing the basis of the foot, solidly upon the ground, on account of the convexity, which we are obliged to give the shoe.

Having hitherto considered the shoeing of feet, in relation to their form, let us now proceed to the shoeing of those, which are very defective in their position.

* See the brass shoe, No. 4.

When

When the toes are turned outwards, the pressure of the foot on the ground lies chiefly on the inward quarters; the farrier's object should be to diminish this pressure, if he can, by increasing it on the outward quarters. He will most likely succeed; 1st. By preserving to the inward quarter all its height. Secondly, by lowering that of the outward quarter. Thirdly, by increasing the thickness of the inward branch of the shoe; and, Fourthly, by rendering the outward one very thin. By means of this two-fold operation, the foot will be brought back to the vertical plane, and will bear equally, and at the same time, on all parts of its circumference.

We should also take care to shoe with great exactness, and very short in the inner heel, because horses, whose feet are turned outwards, are apt to cut themselves with the extremity of the inner branch. And here we must observe, that if the defect under consideration, has its origin in the upper parts of the extremity, or in the too narrow conformation of the chest, as it sometimes happens, we

must

must renounce the method we have just laid down: because, by suddenly altering the position of the foot, though a vicious one, we should expose the ligaments of the articulations, between that part and the shoulder, to hurtful extensions, of more dangerous consequence than the fault which we meant to correct: it is therefore only, when that fault proceeds from the articulation of the fetlock, that some attempt may be made by a slow and gradual process.

When the toes are turned inwardly, one must proceed by a contrary method. 1st. Cut the inward quarter. Secondly, preserve the outward one. Thirdly, increase the thickness of the branch on that side; and, Fourthly, diminish that of the inward branch, by taking off as much as possible from the wall, reckoning from the middle of the toe to the middle of the inward quarter; because it is with this part that the horse cuts himself: but before we employ this method, we must understand the nature of the fault, and for that purpose we must employ the mode of reasoning used in the former article.

Q   We

We proceed now to the consideration of the narrow heel; or, as the farriers call it, hoof bound: this defect consists in the excessive contraction of the heels and quarters, and is natural to many horses of the southern parts of Europe, and also to blood horses of different countries. There is no remedy against this original defect. We must pare and shoe the foot, as if it were a good one, and apply the concave shoe, which will project rather more, than in a well formed foot. By these means, we shall stop the progress of this defect, which the farriers promote by cutting away the sole, the frog, and the binders.

This, when not an original defect, proceeds from the naturally dry disposition of the fibres or the hoof; from the destruction of the sole, the frog, and the binders; as also from the concave or hollow shape of the upper surface of the shoe; but the natural dryness of the fibres alone, however great, seldom produces lameness. It is then the butress, that butchering tool, that almost always occasions this evil we

are

are speaking of. It is very rare for a hoof-bound foot to be perfectly restored; but the defect may be diminished, or at least its progress stopped.

To this end the sole, the frog, and binders, must be preserved with the utmost care. These parts in their growth will throw out the heels a little, or at least will form an opposition to their further contraction.

The heels are to be pared flat, as well as the whole circumference of the wall; and we must use the common concave shoe, and in order to second the effects of shoeing, we must not omit bathing the feet in luke-warm water, and applying emollient poultices both under and over the foot. We must not expect a speedy cure; the space of a year is a very short term in a case of this nature, as may be judged by considering the slowness of the reproduction of the nail.

I cannot pass over in silence the slipper shoe, which many practitioners use to remedy the defect in question.

tion, and which is at present the only resource of the professors of the veterinary schools in France. The shape of this shoe is exactly the same as that of the common shoe in the whole extent of its surface; but the outward edge is exceedingly thin, whilst the inward is altogether as thick; so that the side of the shoe towards the foot, forms a slope, of which the pretended use is, to press open the heels, and turn them outwards. But not only nature will not consent to so forced an effect, but we must also observe, that we really encrease the cause of the defect, in opening the heels, as the farriers do, in order to apply this slipper shoe.*

Let us now proceed to the shoeing of a horse, *that cuts*, as it is called. We have already said, in speaking of feet, that, turned inwards or outwards, the horse cuts himself with the toes or with the

---

* This particular error alone, under which farriers labour, will make it evident how necessary it is to be acquainted with the nature of the thing on which we are employed; and recals the apt remark of Vegetius, " Curare rationabiliter non potest, qui qualitatem rei quam curat ignora·."

heels.

heels. This accident happens more or less frequently, in proportion to the degree of defect in the
conformation, and of weakness or weariness in the
horse. In all these cases, there is but one remedy,
which consists in applying a shoe perfectly exact,
very short on the inner side, and without stamp-
holes on that side, and paring off from the quarters
as much as possible without destroying it, as frequently happens. Several farriers, unable to succeed
by this simple method, give to the inward branch of
the shoe several irregular forms, which, without preventing the evil, make the feet bear foul on the
ground.

By just attending to the following reflections, we
shall be convinced of the uselessness of the excessive thickness which some farriers give to the inward branch of the shoe; and of the cramps which
others raise on some points of that branch.

It is certainly not when the foot is on the ground,
that it cuts the neighbouring leg, it is only when
that

that foot is up; consequently, whatever position we give the foot, by means of any shape whatever of the shoe, we shall never be able to change the action or play of the muscles, nor the direction of the articulated parts of the leg.

It is possible, by the manner of shoeing, to turn the toes a little inwards, or a little outwards, and consequently the heels also: but this effect will only last, while the foot rests upon the ground; as soon as it quits it, it must follow the direction given by the leg, and form a curve, larger or smaller, which brings it nearer to the supporting leg, and which it will strike every time that the horse happens to close his equilibrium in going; the only remedy, therefore, is to shoe to a nicety, inwardly.

We shall now endeavour to explain, concisely, the causes which occasion a horse to over-reach, i. e. to strike his hind upon his fore feet, and to indicate the best method of shoeing in that case.

The

The act of over-reaching is performed by the toes of the hind feet striking the shoes of the fore feet, either on, or between its branches, or else by striking the heels, which are thereby often dangerously cut, or bruised. It is obvious, that the hind feet could not strike the fore feet, unless these last remained too long on the ground, or unless the former rose from it too soon, this tardiness in the one, or over quickness in the other, is the effect of the particular conformation of the horse, though sometimes the fault of the rider, sometimes of the farrier.

Horses most liable to over-reach are those, which are low in front, with large shoulders, and a bulky head; and the neck either too long or too thick: In all these cases, the fore legs being overburthened, rise but with difficulty, and not sufficiently, and cover very little ground. It is useless to observe, that a horse is also subject to over-reach, when he's too high in his hind quarters, because this height is only determined by his being too low in front. A horse over-reaches also, when his fore legs stand un-

der

der him, i. e. when they are in an oblique direction, inclining backwards, or when the hinder extremities approach too near the centre of gravity of the body, whether it proceeds from the general direction of the limb, or merely from too great a bend in the hock. A horse over-reaches, when he is too short in the body; when the spine or back bone is curved out-wards.   A horse may also over-reach from acciden-tal causes, as when a rider overburthens the shoul-ders of his horse with his own weight; this fault is very common in England, and indeed there is no country where horses are so soon ruined before.*

The neglect of the hand in abandoning the bridle, may dispose a horse to over-reach; when the toe of the hind shoe, and the heel of the fore shoe are

---

* This remark is only directed to the abuse of the thing. Every good rider must be sensible, that the forward inclination which he gives his body in galloping, with the design of equalizing his weight between the fore and hind quarters, may be so abused by a bad rider, as to throw the weight on the shoulders. and thus overburthen them; and that this is really the case, appears by an attentive investigation of the subject.

too

too long, it promotes the action of over-reaching.
Lastly, the natural laziness of a horse will expose
him to the same inconvenience.

To remedy the action of over-reaching, we must
endeavour to accelerate the rising of the fore feet,
and to retard that of the hind, in which we sometimes succeed by the following means.

Begin by cutting and paring the fore heels, as
much as possible, without weakening them, and
then use the half moon shoe, No. 1, of which the
heels are very short and thin; on the contrary, preserve all the height of the hind heels, take off as
much of the toe as possible, and shoe very short in
this part. The shoe No. 2, may fulfil this object.
The effect, which the manner of paring may produce, deserves to be explained.

The height of the fore heels being diminished,
will expose the flexor muscles to a greater extension; from whence will proceed a degree of uneasi-

R   ness

ness, which will oblige the horse to lift its foot from the ground, sooner than it would have done, had the heels been higher. In the hind feet, on the contrary, not only the whole height of the heels will be preserved, but an addition made thereto; and from the thickness of the shoe, the last degree of extension of the flexor muscles will be retarded. The horse, far from being induced through pain to take his hind leg from the ground, will keep it there longer than if his heels had been lower, and from this manner of operating there will result a greater interval of time, between the motion of the fore and hind legs, which will oppose itself to the action of over-reaching. A very simple comparison will probably render this principle very intelligible.

Women, who wear very high heeled shoes, walk, almost all, with their knees more or less bent, so that the extensor muscles never attain the last degree of contraction, nor the flexors the last degree of extension, which the construction of the leg would allow of.

But

But should they suddenly change the shoes they have been accustomed to for some with very low heels, they would first experience a painful stretching in the last mentioned muscles, which would oblige them to lift their feet sooner from the ground, than in the former case.

It will doubtless be observed, that as the application of the principles here establised to prevent a horse from over-reaching, produces pain, it cannot be agreeable to nature;* this I admit, and I therefore recommend acting in this case with all possible prudence in the beginning.

The late M. Bourgelat, whose theory did not always agree with his practice, had imagined different

* This however, is not so solid an objection, as may at first appear. When applied to an old horse, it is valid in all its extent; but it is otherwise in a young horse who may have shewn this disposition when breaking. At that age, the carriage of the body, and the position of the feet, may be as successfully corrected as among mankind, where education improves and almost alters the form of individuals; and though attended with some uneasiness in infancy, is presently converted into nature.

R 2   methods

methods of shoeing, relative to the different conformation of horses; such as that of a horse too long
in the body, either from the too great length of the
thorax, or by the extension of the *os ileum*; or of a
horse too short in the body, or of one too low, &c.

But the process employed in the different circumstances, tends to encrease the defect intended to be
corrected, and would ruin the foot, and even the
whole limb, before it produced the effect, which we
might flatter ourselves to obtain. We shall therefore banish from our practice all operations built on
chimerical foundations, and confine ourselves to such
only, as experience, concurring with nature, daily
confirms.

M. Bourgelat also calls in all the assistance of
mechanics, in order to explain, how a foot that does
not wear out the shoe evenly, ought to be shod; and
he divides the under surface of the foot, by a longi-
tudinal axis, traverse axis, diagonal, &c. I am persuaded, I shall sooner explain myself to the farrier's
common

common sense, by saying to him, when a horse is brought you to be shod, examine the old shoe, and see what part is most worn out. If it is the outward branch, preserve the quarter on that side, and encrease the thickness of the shoe at that part; you will by this means remedy the fault: besides, particular cases occur every day, which it is impossible to foresee, and which require the shoe to be differently shaped. As for instance, when the quarter or heel has been destroyed, the foot wounded or pricked, the sole compressed or burnt, &c. In such cases, as it is not in our power to lay down fixed and certain rules; the operator, guided by the actual state of the foot, must give the shoe, or some of its parts, a shape adapted to the affected part, and qualified to assist its healing. As to the half-moon shoe, semi-half-moon shoe, &c. we shall mention them in treating of those cases, in which they are to be used; and we shall now briefly recapitulate the substance of this lecture, addressing ourselves to all farriers, who are able and willing to understand us.

You,

You, whose office it is to shoe the valuable creature, which is the subject of our enquiries, should abandon that blind and perverse custom, by which you destroy that essential part, the preservation of which is entrusted to your care; and submitting your understandings to the light of reason and experience, should endeavour to obtain a knowledge of those principles, on which the perfection of your art depends, and which alone can lead you to a sound and luminous practice. Lay aside, in the first place, the mechanical custom of paring the foot to excess, of thinning the sole and frog; and destroying the binders, under the false idea of opening the heels, which, on the contrary, you by that means dispose to contract; of cutting away their hind part, which is the most solid point of rest that nature has provided for the foot. Recollect, in short, that you are only to take off from this part, that portion of the old horn, which would impair the solidity of the shoe. In the next place, you are to imitate with the shoe the concave form of the foot. Let this same shoe fit exactly the circumference of the wall, without

out compelling the latter, as you are accustomed to
do, to fit the shape of the shoe.   Beware of making
the under part of the shoe convex, excepting in the
case of a convex foot.   Above all, avoid turning the
branches of the shoe obliquely outwards, because
this distortion pinches the quarters and heels, and
finally crushes them.   Reduce the thickness of the
heels of the shoe: be persuaded, that when they are
too thick, they raise the frog too much above the
ground, and that then the horse is in the same case,
as you would be, if obliged to walk on tiptoe.   You
cannot but be sensible, how much this last fault
must contribute to ruin the legs. . Lastly, never rasp
the surface of the hoof above the rivets.

By adopting the method here delineated, you will
at least avoid the grosser errors, which are every day
committed, and if you have sufficient courage to
give yourselves up to the study necessary for acquiring the true principles of your art, public opinion
will soon place you on a level with men who are
enlightened, and therefore useful to society.

LECTURE IV.

_____

On the Natural and Accidental Diseases of the Foot.

As I esteem it my duty to quote those authors with whom my principles coincide, in consequence, I shall begin this lecture with the literal description which M. Lafosse gives of that well known disease called the *Bleime*, or corns, reserving to myself, nevertheless, the privilege of making some observations upon it : he expresses himself in the following manner.

" The *Bleime* is a redness in the sole of the heels,
" and is of two sorts, the one natural, the other ac-
" cidental, the natural sort comes without any appa-
" rent cause, in feet with large heels, and is of four
" kinds.

" In

" In the first there appears a redness, produced
" by extravasated blood dried up in the pores of the
" horny sole.

" In the second, there, appears in the horny part
" which is split, a black spot like the prick of a nail,
" and, on examination, the channelled or laminated
" flesh appears black and putrid.

" In the third kind, on paring the part, matter is
" observed to issue from the channelled flesh in
" the heels.

" In the fourth, an opening or separation is ob-
" served on paring, between the wall and the soles
" of the heels, caused by the matter, which is black,
" and in a small quantity.

" To these four kinds may be added a fifth, in
" which the wall of the heels is reversed to the
" form of an oyster-shell, which. bearing inwardly,
" compresses the channelled flesh of the heels.
" These

" These kinds of feet have no binder, and but very
" little sole, easily yielding to the pressure of the
" fingers.

" The accidental *Bleime* is caused by bad shoeing;
" low heels, bearing upon the shoes, are thereby com-
" pressed and bruised; they may, in like manner,
" suffer from gravel lodged between the shoe and
" the heels, particularly after the foot has been
" pared. A bruise is the cause of this sort of *Bleime*,
" to remedy which the foot must be short shoed,
" and not pared, and thin at the heels, that the frog
" may totally and equally bear upon the ground.

" In the second sort, where the black spot is ob-
" served in the angle of the binder, and where the
" foliated flesh is putrid, an opening must be made
" with the butress, and pledgets steeped in spirits
" of turpentine introduced, which is to be held in a
" state of compression, lest the foliated flesh should
" rise above it. In the third kind, where in paring
" matter is observed to issue from the furrowed

" flesh

" flesh of the heels, recourse must be had to other
" means.

" The fifth results from a natural defect in the
" formation of the foot; the heels have scarcely any
" binders, the *Bleime* is barely covered by the horny
" substance, the horse is very tender in that part,
" because the wall is inverted, and pinches the foli-
" ated flesh; this unnatural growth of the horn must
" be cut with the butress. Sometimes it suppurates,
" in which case, an opening must be made to give
" the matter a free issue, with care not to make it
" too large, lest the flesh should rise in a lump,
" called in French, *cerise* or cherry; the dressing
" consists in pledgets, laid one over the other, in or-
" der to support the flesh, which naturally falls." It
would be difficult to give a better description of the
Bleime, or to prescribe a more proper method of
treating it; but I must observe that M. Lafosse, in
the design of rendering himself perspicuous, multi-
plies the divisions to such a degree, as to make them
appear, to persons but little instructed, so many distinct disorders.

I do not entirely agree with M. Lafosse, on the cause of the *Bleime*, nor do I believe it so frequently proceeds from nature as he does; we sometimes meet with it indeed in feet whose heels are too hard, but not so often as could be supposed, after the description which he gives of it; besides, Arabian, Barbary, Turkish, Spanish, and Navarine horses, in general all horses of southern countries, are more subject to this sort of *Bleime* than the northern, because their feet are naturally harder, and of a drier nature than the latter.

Low heels, with scarcely any binders, are, says he, subject to the natural Bleime. I am, on the contrary, of opinion, that although this vicious conformation is the predisposing cause, that the *Bleime* is always determined by some immediate cause, either by the pressure of the shoe, or by gravel or stones lodged between the branches and the sole, in proof of which I am thoroughly convinced, that it is possible, by the mode of shoeing alone, to prevent this disease in feet, whose heels are low and feeble. To avoid

avoid perplexing the minds of those who wish to study the diseases of the feet, I shall omit all superfluous divisions, in stating, that a simple corn is at first observed by a redness in the part of the sole, situated between the heels and the binders, and that its progress is in proportion to the cause which gave rise to it. In consequence, a black spot is sometimes observed, which announces that the quick or living parts are more or less affected, and in paring the foot, a black sanies or gore is often noticed, which has destroyed the fleshy sole in this place, and even the foliated substance, so as to have excavated the wall, from whence results the inversion of the quarter. I have found, by experience, that M. Lafosse's method is the best to be followed in treating this disease.

I shall here assume the liberty of making a few observations on the general mode of farriers in operating for this disease. The chief care to be taken in paring the foot, is to preserve, as much as possible, the heels, the quarters, and the binders. On the

the contrary, these begin by cutting away all the parts, without reflecting on the length of time which nature requires in order to re-produce them. The operator is then obliged to erect a purchase in the room of that he had destroyed, for which reason he lays on the bar-shoe, upon which the frog is obliged to perform the office of the heels. This shoe is almost always ill shaped, and too heavy, and ruins the foot instead of easing it; whereas, if the farrier skilfully preserved the parts which he ignorantly destroys, he would avoid the use of this shoe, and employ the half moon shoe, No. 6,* which by leaving the frog and heels free, would facilitate the growth of the latter.

But we cannot expect to establish one method, by criticising another; let us therefore look back, and see whether we have not exposed ourselves to some censure. Some people, I foresee, may object to the half moon shoe, as impracticable in a country where the roads are covered with flinty sharp gravel, which

* See the brass shoe, No. 6.

would

would inevitably destroy the naked heels.   This objection would be reasonable, without doubt, if the
horse was put to work immediately after the operation; but every man of sense, who will keep his
horse at rest until his heels shall have acquired a little consistence and strength, will soon clearly see, in
this circumstance, the advantage of the method I
propose.

Let us now examine that disease, called seime or
sand crack, which means a cleft more or less visible,
when the animal rests his foot on the ground.

The best method of preventing sand cracks in dry
feet, is to keep the fibres which compose the hoof
pliant, particularly near the coronet; this can be effected by the use of emollient baths, made with a
decoction of mallows, or with simple water, and by
the application of poultices of the same quality, composed of mallows, marsh-mallows, pellitory of the
wall, &c.

In

In this particular instance, the use of greasy, oily ointments is to be rejected. Farriers, and particularly grooms, use them frequently with the intention of rendering the foot more pliant, and to blacken the hoof, and only exercising a comparative instinct, attribute to these oily substances, the faculty of softening, nourishing, and relaxing the horny substance of the hoof, for no other reason, than because they see them produce the effect upon the leather harnesses of their horses. If it were possible to persuade them that oily and fat substances applied to organized parts, obstruct the pores, and oppose the passage of insensible perspiration, and excite inflammation and suppuration, they might be induced to abandon their old practice, but the undertaking would prove difficult, and more than doubtful. I should think the most probable method to succeed in convincing them of so pernicious a practice, would be, by forbiding absolutely the use of any sort of oily, greasy ointment, and refusing to pay for these expensive articles, by visiting the stables from time to time, with a view of examining the horses feet, and

T   finally

finally by discharging any groom who should infringe these orders.

But the abject state veterinary medicine is in, together, with that blind and unlimited confidence which masters place in servants, will yet for a long time resist this salutary reformation, till we learn to distinguish between science and ignorance, between the man of acquired knowledge, and elaboratory study, and the illiterate stable boy. I cannot forbear inserting here, an advertisement which appeared in one of the public papers, and which evidently proves the actual state of the science. " Wanted, a man and a boy, a father and son would be preferable, the man must be perfectly well acquainted with the nature and care of horses, in breaking, nicking, and physicking, he must be able and willing to do all kind of out door work."

If it can be imagined that a servant may possess the knowledge of Hippocrates, it would be wrong to place any confidence in physicians, whose advice is

attended

attended with great expence ; would it not be better to advertise for a servant properly qualified to dress hair, shave, bleed, prescribe a purge, and even to cut a leg or an arm off, if his master should have occasion? The latter has an equal right to skill in physic, as the former to the veterinary art, and ought, in consequence, to be invested with the same privileges. A similar parallel may be drawn between the shoemaker and the farrier.

I proceed now to the consideration of a very stubborn disease, in the treatment of which, farriers are generally baffled; it is called in French, *fic* or *crapaud*, and it is known in English by the appellation of canker.

This disease more frequently affects the hind than the fore feet, the causes which give rise to it, may be divided into internal and external; the external cause displays itself by the excessive height and thickness of the heels, in feet whose frog, though naturally but of little bulk, is yet compressed on

T 2 both

both sides.   The continuance of the acrid and irritating mud in the inward part of the foot, the continual soaking of the feet in urine and dung; all these
causes are assisted by the butress, which by destroying the covering of the frog, exposes it to the action
of the acrid particles to which it is exposed.

The inward causes are all such things as vitiate
the humours, direct them to the legs, and give rise
to the obstinate disorder, which we call the running
thrush.   These humours often acquiring a great degree of acrimony, and even becoming corrosive, fall
upon the frog and there produce the canker.   The
danger attending it, is greater or less, according to
the parts affected; when the frog, and the flesh only
are affected, and the disease not deeply rooted, the
cure will be effected with no great difficulty, but
sometimes it makes such ravages, as to invade the
aponeurosis of the flexor muscle of the foot, and
even the bone itself, where it sometimes takes root,
and extends its progress between the quarters, it
then separates them, by destroying the fleshy sole
                                                    near-

near the heels, as well as the foliated or laminated substance, and even the posterior part of the cartilage is not always secured from its attack.

That we may not confound the canker in its origin with other excrescences, which may rise in the frog, or near the heels, we must examine its substance, which for the most part is filementous or thread like, soft, presenting numberless small excrescences, resembling little mushrooms, but very slender. Its existence once ascertained, we should not confine ourselves to the common methods used by farriers, which consist in the application of caustics, with the intention of burning them off, these insufficient means consume only the surface, but leave the root which will constantly re-produce the disease. To obtain a perfect cure, it will first be necessary to examine whether the horse is troubled with the running thrush, whether the cracks exist only in the folds of the pastern; and whether an acrid humour issues from the part. In all these circumstances, we should first endeavour to remove the disorder,

which

which is the primitive cause of the fic, and not attempt to cure the disease itself, before we have freed
the leg from every kind of discharge; we are then
not to be satisfied with a superficial treatment; we
must therefore begin, by putting the horse on low
diet for two or three days, to prevent a fever, which
is often attended with danger; he must be blooded,
and a few emollient glysters injected, made with a
decoction of mallows, and every day he must swallow three or four quarts of a cooling mash, composed
of a decoction of the root of marsh-mallows, with
three or four drachms of nitre dissolved in each
mash.

The horse being thus prepared, the operation of
unsoling is to be performed, by which means we
may the more easily discover the part affected.
The instrument employed in this operation, is called
the sage leaf, with which the canker must be eradi-
cated, by making a deep incision to its very roots,
whether it affects the fleshy substance of the frog,
the aponeurosis of the flexor muscle, the laminated

or

or foliated flesh, the cartilages, or even if it penetrates to the bone of the foot; but as the cartilaginous, aponeurotic, and bony parts will admit of no
cure, without exfoliation, the application of an actual,
cautery to the extremities of the parts that may.
have been effected, either by the disorder or the
instrument, will be found requisite.

After the operation, pledgets, moistened with;
tincture of myrrh and aloes, or the traumatic balsam,.
may be laid over the cauterised parts, the rest of the
surface of the wound is to be dressed with a pledget:
dipped in the æthereal spirit of turpentine, and the
apparatus so managed, as to make an equal compression on all the parts.

If the operation should have been long and painful, the horse must be blooded again, plenty of;
blanched water given him to drink, and but little
solid food. Three or four days after the operation,.
the wound is to be dressed for the first time; two
days after, the dressing is to be renewed, and examination

nation made, whether suppuration has taken place, of what quality it is. If a kind of red serum appears, it is a proof that the root of the fic was not totally destroyed, and recourse must be had immediately to a second operation, which must be carried deeper than at first, that no vestiges of the affected part may remain. If in dressing the wound, the flesh appears to rise, and to become soft and proud, apply a digestive, made with the yolk of egg, turpentine, oil of hypericum, and a sufficient quantity of powdered vitriol, to check the over rapid growth of the flesh.

It would be useless here to observe, that a perfect exfoliation of the aponeurotic, cartilaginous, and bony parts must take place; without this, the scar would prove deceitful, and the canker would in time spring up again. In the mean time, we are to be apprehensive of a symptomatic fever, which is always to be feared, during the cure of this disease.

The

The next evil, which demands our utmost attention, is one of the most rebellious, incident to the foot, and which requires the most anatomical knowledge in the operation necessary for its cure. This in French is called *javart*, in English the horny quitter; it may be produced by different causes, such as a blow or violent contusion in the coronet, which produces an inflammation, suppuration, or a caries of the cartilage; a deep crack neglected or ill treated, which, penetrating to the cartilage, affects it grievously; a corn, the matter of which finding no passage through the sole, forces its way up between the quarter and the foot bone, by destroying the foliated substance, invades the cartilage, and opens itself a passage in the coronet: an acrimonious humour detained in the part, may give rise to the quitter; or the sudden suppression of the perspiration; or it may be produced by the mud of great towns, composed of iron, urine and other corrosive principles capable of producing this disease, which we may compare with the third species of whitlow in man.

A fresh

A fresh quitter, which has not as yet affected the cartilage iseasily cured; it requires no other treatment than that of simple wounds, but when in its progress it has penetrated into the interior of the foot, so that the cartilaginous parts are affected, the cure becomes difficult, and even doubtful, because it is requisite to extirpate all the parts which the pus has rotted.

Farriers, unacquainted with the anatomical organization of the foot, can form no idea of the surgical operation which this disease requires; it is even lucky they do not attempt it, for of one hundred horses, probably ninety-nine would be for ever lamed, and perhaps the whole number; their method extends no farther than the application of caustics, searing points, and fire stripes; all these local applications, whose effects reach no farther than the surface, are absolutely insufficient; and while the farrier is amusing himself in burning off the fungus's of the exterior wound with vitriol, &c. the matter is making such a rapid progress inwardly in the foot, as to render the quitter incurable. This observation is

founded

founded on daily facts, and it is easy to prove, that not a week passes, without seeing some horses labouring under these incurable diseases, led to the slaughtering houses; let us, however, suppose a horse attacked with the most grievous quitter.

The veterinarian is to begin to probe the wound, by dexterously following the direction and depth of the fistulas formed by the pus in the foot, and he is to endeavour to find out if the cartilage be affected; but as it may sometimes prove impossible to judge exactly of the irregular bottoms of the wound, he ought to determine to proceed to the operation, previously observing the following precautions; let him begin by reducing his food, and giving him plenty of blanched water to drink; let the foot be pared, and the quarter rasped thin, near where the operation is to be made, and the foot be wrapped up in an emollient poultice, during two or three days. The horse. thus prepared, must be tied and thrown on a litter of straw, and a ligature bound round his pastern, to prevent an hæmorrhage; an incision is then to be

made

made with a bistoury parallel with the coronet, and long enough to be able to discover the cartilage in all its extent; more or less of the superior part of the wall is to be cut away, as occasion may require, but the inferior part of the quarter, as well as the heel, should be preserved, to serve as a fulcrum, or purchase for the foot, unless the state of the disease requires it otherwise; then let him change the instrument, called the sage leaf, with a blunt back, and slightly bent, with which, let him cut away the cartilage gradually, at three or four different attempts. It is in this conjecture, that the anatomical knowledge of the foot is of great and indispensable assistance, particularly, while the operator is passing his instrument behind the cartilage; because this part covers the principal blood vessels of the foot, as well as the capsular ligament of its articulation, with the bone of the coronet, an accidental opening or breach of which would lame the horse for ever.

But however dexterous a person may be in extirpating the cartilage with the sage leaf, some portions

of

of the root of it, which are inserted in the bone of the foot, will still remain; these must be taken away with a scraping knife, which must be managed with all dexterity possible, observing to fix this instrument on a solid part, and gently bearing from within outwards, to avoid opening the capsular ligament, which is very near the parts in which the operation is performed. After the last portion of the cartilage is taken away, let him examine whether the bone of the foot be carious; if it should be so, let him remove the carious part, and apply an actual cautery, in order to facilitate the exfoliation.

In fine, having ended all these proceedings, let him inspect minutely into the bottom of the wound, to ascertain whether any sinus or fistula remain, and when the operation is completely performed, let him lay on the first dressing, which consists in applying to the bottom of the wound small pledgets, soaked in a mixture of brandy and vinegar, or spirits of turpentine. These dressings must be so disposed, as to make an equal, but sufficient compression on all the surface

surface they cover; and let him finish the dressing, by laying over the wound, and round the coronet, larger pledgets, to avoid compressing that part, which must be carefully attended to. The bandage consists of a piece of linen almost square, and big enough to go round the pastern and the foot; and a roller three ells in length, or there about, and two inches in breadth, the whole being skilfully laid on, the horse is to be led back to the stable, limping on his three legs, and afterwards the ligature to be taken off. It is necessary to bleed him in the jugular vein to prevent a fever, which most commonly succeeds so painful an operation; it is likewise essentially necessary to keep the patient to his blanched water, and to supply him sparingly with food for a few days.

The first dressing is to be taken off at the end of a week, but without examining the wound, or trying to probe it, least an hæmorrhage should ensue. The second dressing is to be taken off after five or six days, at which time the suppuration will begin to take place,

place, unless the wound has been too strongly compressed, and it is to be dressed in the same manner as at first. In three or four days more, the third dressing is to be taken off, when the veterinarian must examine, if there are any black spots upon the surface of the wound, which is commonly a proof that the cartilage has not been totally taken away. In this case another slight operation must be had recourse to, to remove entirely the small particles that may have remained; afterwards the wound is to be dressed every other day, with the same digestive, excepting the parts which have been cauterised, upon which small pledgets dipped in tincture of myrrh and aloes, are to be laid as a spirituous dissicative, to accelerate the exfoliation, which most commonly happens within forty or fifty days, though I have seen it not take place in a month; but this depends upon the age and constitution of the animal.

When the escar has fallen off, the wound soon fills up, but it is essentially necessary, as has been observed, to be assured of a perfect exfoliation; for if

any

dead particles of the cartilage, or of the bone, should remain, they would give rise to fistulas, make the cicatrization imperfect, and occasion a second operation.

To prevent so unfortunate a repetition, it will be necessary, at every dressing, to examine the wound with the greatest attention, and to see if no livid black spots are observable in it, which furnish a greater supply of matter, than the wound itself; probe these spots, and if the exfoliation be not judged complete, introduce a sufficiently solid tent, imbibed with the aloetic and myrrh tincture, and lightly dust it over with powdered vitriol, in order, on the one part, to facilitate the separation of the non-exfoliated portion, and on the other, to consume part of the flesh which covers it: when once the bottom of the wound is expunged and clean, it assumes the appearance of a simple wound, and a perfect cicatrice will make ample amends for all your trouble.

LECTURE

LECTURE V.

FOUNDERING.

THE most severe and stubborn disease, to which the horse's foot is liable, and which is almost ever fatal, unless subdued in its origin, is beyond a doubt, that which is known under the name of foundering. It is to be considered as a fluxion, more or less inflammatory, which has its seat more particularly in the interior of the foot.

This disease manifests itself by the following symptoms, which may be divided into common, and particular. The former are pain and heat in the feet, especially at the coronet; fulness or plethora in the vessels of the legs; a strong pulsation in that

x   part;

part; a swelling in the sheath of the tendons, and also a symptomatic fever, when the disease becomes serious; whence result sadness, and a distaste for solid food; but the latter symptoms only appear, when the pain and inflammation are increased to a very intense degree.

The particular symptoms appear in the step of the animal when walking, and in the position of the legs when standing still. If a horse, for instance, is foundered in his two fore feet, the great pain he feels in those parts, obliges him to throw back the weight of his body upon his hinder extremities, in such a manner as to bring them forward very near to the centre of gravity; whilst the fore legs remain in an oblique direction, inclining from before backwards. In this position, the loins of the animal are in a state of continual exertion, and if forced to walk, he experiences great difficulty in moving, and his fore legs do not quit the ground, till his hind ones are brought very far forward under his body, the whole weight of which, they are obliged to sustain.

tain. This painful translation of the body, obliges the horse to bend the spine, and this forced action in the vertebræ of the loins, persuades many farriers, that the seat of the disease exists in the muscles of the back and loins, on which they apply remedies of all kinds, the effects of which, as may be imagined, are always useless, and often dangerous.

This treatment, erroneous in its principle, and unsuccessful in its issue, determines the farrier to draw a consequence evidently false, by supposing that the disease has changed its place, and is fallen into the feet.

When the foundering is in the hind feet, the animal stands in a position directly opposite to that we have been describing. He carries his body forward, with his head low, and the anterior extremities under him, by which means the withers become lower than the croup; in short, the attitude of all the parts proves, that nature is engaged in easing the hind feet, by throwing the weight of the mass upon the fore-feet.

X 2 But

But as the hinder extremities are always particularly employed in projecting the body, it is easy to conceive how very painful this effort must be to the horse, since it is only with the fore legs, that he is now able to effect it.   And, in fact, it is easy to perceive the state of constraint under which the horse labours, when he displaces one of his fore legs; he hesitates some time before he moves it, and he has hardly taken it up, before he speedily replaces it on the ground, and during this action the tremor and vacillation of the other other fore-leg, denotes the excess of weight which distresses it.

This disease is rendered dangerous by the painful, and forced state of the parts, inducing a considerable degree of fever, which announces itself, as in all inflammatory cases, by the hardness and quickness of the pulse; the heat of the mouth, attended with unnatural thirst, partial sweatings often appear in the neck, near the shoulders, between the fore-legs, as also in the flanks, &c.

Foundering

Foundering sometimes attacks all the four legs, and when that happens, the horse is unable to stand; he therefore is constantly lying down; and I have seen one that placed himself on his back, in order to find ease. It is uncommon for this distemper to attack one foot only, either before or behind. Some authors have multiplied the causes of this disease almost to infinity; they have supposed some to be hereditary; others they endeavour to explain by the aid of physiological systems, which sound reason can never adopt. We shall confine ourselves to the exposition of those only which experience appears to confirm every day.

The most dangerous cause of all is a suppression of the perspiration; this commonly occasions a great inflammation in the feet, the progress of which is exceedingly rapid, the superabundance of blood, its thickness, the vitiated disposition of the humours may increase the intensity of the fluxion, and render its resolution more difficult.

Violent

Violent galloping, or too hard labour may occasion foundering; it may also proceed from too much rest, and it is not uncommon to find a horse in this state, on his being brought out of a stable, where he has remained too long without exercise. It has further been observed, that any abundant evacuation, such as much bleeding, sometimes produces this disorder; it is also frequently owing to the use of too nourishing a food, and too liberally bestowed, such as lucerne, sainfoin, clover, barley, beans, vetches, peas, &c.

Bad shoeing often produces the distemper we are treating of; the farriers, by scooping the sole to excess, occasion it to dry up, facilitate the contraction of the heels, and the shoe which they use being too narrow and concave at top, completes the contraction of the whole circumference of the foot.*

If

* It is worthy of remark, that the writers in the Geoponica, and in the collection of Ruellius, Varro, Columella, and Vegetius; that is to say, all those who wrote before the use of the iron shoe, dwell very little on the diseases of the feet, especially the severer diseases
mentioned

If in this state of constraint, the horse is obliged to tread on dry hard ground, the heat increases, inflammation succeeds, and foundering is the consequence. This distemper may also be the consequence of a painful operation; but as several of the causes we have been describing are opposite in their natures, they must necessarily occasion a difference in the disease they produce; and it is on this account that foundering is attended with more or less inflammation, according to the principle which gave rise to it. It ought, therefore, to be treated according to the symptoms which characterise it.

mentioned in this and the foregoing lecture; which fact furnishes a very fair ground of inference, that the method of shoeing now in use, may be considered as a principal cause of those evils. Indeed, when we consider how very delicate, and at the same time, how very important a part of the animal machine the foot is, when we reflect how absolutely the hoof is compelled to obey the form of the shoe, whether it favours or counteracts the original designs of nature in its formation; when we add to these considerations the mischief which a wrong direction given to a single nail must occasion, or an ignorant use of the instrument with which farriers weaken or impair the natural armour of the foot; and finally, if we subjoin the education of those to whom custom has hitherto committed this important trust, and the quality of the art they profess, we shall be well prepared to receive the conclusive proof which experience will furnish, that these causes have considerably augmented the number of diseases of the feet.

I shall

I shall proceed to give a literal account of the treatment which the veterinary schools of the Continent advantageously employ in the case of foundering. Having practised it myself, with success, I recommend it in preference to any other, because I believe it to be the result of the most mature consideration, and the best adapted to cases and circumstances.

The treatment of this disorder is divided into internal and external; I shall begin with the first. When foundering proceeds from the rarefaction of the fluids, frequent and plentiful bleeding will operate with effect in the beginning of the complaint, as also salts dissolved in a decoction of acrid plants. To this end take of sorrel leaves four handfuls, of wild endive two handfuls, of common salt four ounces, salt of nitre one ounce, boil these in two quarts of water; take it off the fire when the sorrel is sufficiently done, pour it out, and give it in two doses, at the interval of an hour.

If

If the distemper is of long standing, and if the fluids are become condensed, which naturally follows their rarefaction, bleeding is recommended, and the salts should be administered, dissolved in sudorific infusions. Take of burdock root four ounces, of fixed alkali one ounce, let them boil a.quarter of an hour in two quarts of water, take them off the fire, add angelica and wild valerian roots of each two ounces, elder flowers one handful, let them infuse two hours, pour the liquor off, and add two ounces of sal ammoniac at the time of giving the draught.

When the condensation is carried to excess, the pure alkaline salts, dissolved in proper infusions, are the only means to be employed. Take of the pure vegetable alkali one drachm, of essence of turpentine two drachms, mix and shake them in a small phial, add this mixture to the first draught of the vegetable decoction described above. These active sudorifics will not operate with less effect when this disorder proceeds from a sudden suppression of the perspiration. In all these cases, we must not omit the use of
Y

diluents,

diluents, which assist the action of these remedies:
accordingly, this draught should be followed by two
or three diluting draughts, if they even only consist
of a simple decoction of mallows.

When a foundering proceeds from too much rest,
it requires less active sudorifics, corresponding to
the progress which the complaint has made; for this
purpose, take of gentian root and rhubarb of each
four drachms, of filings of steel two drachms, bruise
them, and let them be boiled in three pints of water
for about 12 or 15 minutes; being taken from the
fire, and infused for two hours, pour it off, and add
of sal ammoniac two ounces, after this draught, give
the purge No. 8. The foundering that arises from
horses having been fed too plentifully with food of a
heating quality, does not admit of bleeding. If the
abdomen is hard, tense, and overloaded, we must
have recourse to the emollient glyster No. 12, and
the purgatives No. 11, which are to be more or less
increased, according to their operation in the draughts
consisting of the infusion of sage and wormwood
No. 5.

No. 5. When however the food has past the stomach, we may venture to bleed, after which we may
give a gentle purge No. 9, or a more active one No.
8, according to the constitution, age, and other circumstances.

Sometimes this disorder appears to arise from a
super-abundance of the fluids of the body, in which
case the use of the evacuants No. 8, are highly necessary, and also the glysters No. 2 ; and if there is
reason to be alarmed at the redundance of the blood
and humours, these medicines should be preceded by
bleeding, and the diluents No. 6.

There are founderings which discover no other
cause or symptom than a pain in the feet; in this
case every attention must be given to the distempered part, and we must immediately remove the
shoe, in order to examine the parts affected; sometimes it is sufficient to protect particular portions of
the sole or heels from the painful compression
which they experience. This first relief being

given

given, we must next have recourse to bleeding, the draughts No. 7, and to nitrous and camphorated glysters No. 12.

To conclude: there are other cases which are caused by accidents, or proceed from excessive pain in some exterior part of the body, often very remote from the feet; cooling draughts, emollient glysters may be given, anodyne poultices and unguents applied to the seat of the pain, is the most proper treatment of this species of the disorder.

Besides the internal treatment, foundering requires a local one of no less importance, the method of which is determined by the actual state of the distempered parts. If the disorder has not yet disfigured the wall of the hoof, if the coronet is not very hot, the vessels of the shank and pastern not very much swelled, and the pain in the foot not very great, we must frequently lead the horse to water, in order to wash and bathe the part; or, what is still better, we must let the extremity soak in cold water,

water, sharpened with vinegar, and a certain quantity of sal ammoniac, No. 16, or acidulated with any concentrated acid, No. 17. The foot is to be taken out, after having soaked an hour and a half or two hours, and the cavity or under part of the foot is to be filled with pledgets of tow or linen steeped in oil of bayberries, very warm, and the coronet the heels, and the wall wrapped up in the poultice No. 15.

(These dressings must be renewed three or four times a day, and it is highly important not to delay the use of them, but to let the internal treatment, and the local treatment for the feet, keep pace with each other.

If the feet are more severely affected, and the parts surrounding the coronet very painful, scarify it vertically and deeply in its whole extent, without fearing even to touch the cartilages; experience has proved, that such incisions, in the direction of the axis of the limbs are not dangerous; then put the

bleeding

bleeding foot into cold water, accidulated with sal ammoniac No. 16, and when the blood is stopped, take them out of the water, and use the dressing as before prescribed.

If the evil has made still greater progress, and if the swelling and laxity of the coronet, the acuteness of the pain, and the bearing on the heels, announce that the vessels of the foliated or laminated substance are ruptured; in this case removing the sole, or even paring part of its horn, would prove exceedingly dangerous, and would promote the loosening or displacing the coffin bone of the foot : we must, on the contrary, leave to that part all the strength allotted to it; but we must, at the same time, proceed to open the wall, by cutting away part of the anterior surface of the hoof, between the coronet and the sole, to the breadth of two fingers.

When this operation is performed, the part is to be suffered to bleed plentifully in the bath No. 17. It must then be withdrawn and dressed as before directed,

directed, observing to fill up the cavity retisuing from the extirpation of the wall, with pledgets steeped in oil of turpentine. It will be easily conceived that if the evil has made still greater progress, if the bone of the foot, for example, is become carious, &c. it would be rashness to undertake the cure, and that such an attempt would be a signal proof of ignorance.

We must observe, however, that there are founderings of old standing, in the cure of which art is not unsuccessful, but it is easy to conceive, that in such cases, the parts contained within the hoof are only confined, and more or less painfully compressed; that they are attended with no fever, or inflammation, either general or particular; the disease in this case is to be considered as chronical, and must be rendered acute, which may easily be done.

To this end the distempered extremities must be rubbed morning and night with essence of turpentine, from the upper part of the shank to the coronet;

net; these frictions are to be repeated the next and the following day. The inflammation and the irritation this treatment excites, often produces, in a very little time, the resolution of the blood and humours, by which the parts contained within the wall were constrained and compressed.

The horse must be walked during the action of the essence of turpentine, and use must be made of the pledgets steeped in the oil of bayberries, within the sole, and of the defensive poultices No. 15. Whatever may be the causes of foundering, or whatever may be its effects, the diet cannot be too strictly attended to. The animals, who labour under it, should only be allowed blanched water No. 14. Solid food must not be admitted, till the progress of the distemper is stopped; and should the disorder have proceeded from the fulness of the humours, the food could not become salutary, till the animal had been previously purged. Walking the horse, however, can only be salutary, when the foundering has disturbed the bone of the foot; in that case the
motion

motion it communicates to the fluids, prevents their stagnation in the vessels, and promotes their resolution.

MEDICAL RECIPES.
DRAUGHTS.
No. I.

℞. Sorrel leaves four handfuls.
Wild endive two ditto.
Common salt four ounces.
Salt of nitre one ditto.

Let them boil in two quarts of water, when sufficiently boiled, pour the decoction from the leaves, add to it the salts, and give it in two doses, at one hour's interval.

No. II.

℞. Burdock root four ounces.
Fixed alkali one ditto.

Let them boil a quarter of an hour in two quarts of water, take it from the fire, add roots of angelica and wild valerian, of each two ounces, elder flowers one handful, let them infuse two hours, then pour off the infusion, and add, when going to administer the draught, of sal ammoniac two ounces.

z

No.

No. III.

℞. Of the volatile alkali one drachm.

Essence of turpentine two drachms.

Mix, and shake these in a small phial, add this mixture to the draft No. 2, and give it immediately.

No. IV.

℞. Gentian root four drachms,

Rhubarb four ditto.

Bruise these ingredients, and boil them in three pints of water, for twelve or fifteen minutes, then take them from the fire, and let them infuse for two hours, and add of sal ammoniac two ounces.

No. V.

℞. Epsom salts four ounces.

Cream of tartar two ounces.

Let them boil a quarter of an hour in two quarts of water, take the solution from the fire, add sage leaves and wormwood two handfuls, let them infuse one hour, pour it off and give it.

No.

No. VI.

℞. Borage.

French mercury.

Pellitory of the wall.

Wild endive, of each one handful.

Salt of nitre one ounce.

Throw the whole into three quarts of boiling water, let them infuse an hour, then pour it off, and give it.

No. VII.

℞. Of the draught No. 6, one quart.

Camphor half an ounce.

Rectified spirits of wine two drachms.

Dissolve the camphor in the spirits and add it to the draught.

No. VIII.

℞. Draught No. 6, one quart.

Powdered aloes one ounce.

Tartarised vinegar four ounces.

Warm it a little, and stir it from time to time till these substances are dissolved and mixed.

No.

No. IX.

℞. Draught No. 6, three quarts.

Tartarised vinegar eight ounces.

Aloes two drachms.

Dissolve and mix as above.

No. X. Glysters.

℞. Decoction No. 6, three pints.

Add of antimonial tartar one drachm.

Dissolve it warm, and give it in a glyster, after the animal has been purged.

No. XI.

℞. The above glyster.

Add aloes two drachms.

Honey four ounces.

Dissolve it warm, and give it as above.

No. XII.

℞. Draught No. 7.

And administer it as a glyster.

No.

No. XIII. A Suppository.

℞. Soap two ounces.

Powdered aloes one ounce.

Beat them together in a marble mortar, and mix them in your hands, and make a roll, which introduce into the rectum.

No. XIV. A Drink.

℞. Common water, one pail full, whiten it with rye meal, and add salt of nitre one ounce.

No. XV. A Poultice.

℞. Soot from the chimney well baked and sifted one pound, mix it with a sufficient quantity of the strongest vinegar that can be procured. This poultice is to be renewed every four hours.

No. XVI. Baths.

℞. Sal ammoniac two ounces.

Sugar of lead four ounces.

The coldest spring water one pail full.

Let the part affected be soaked in this bath during one hour:

hour : the same bath may serve several times, taking care, before it is used, to immerse the vessel in which it is contained into cold spring water, in order to cool it.

No. XVII.

℞. Spring water one pail full.

Add of the vitriolic acid four ounces.

And let the part soak as above.

A foundering often resists both the efforts of nature and of art. I shall subjoin to the account here given of this distemper, the following observations.

If the treatment that has been prescribed does not stop the progress of the disease, and if it does not produce a resolution of the humours, it will terminate with more or less dreadful effects, according to the age, constitution, and other circumstances of the animal.

Sometimes the inflammation is so rapid, that a total falling off, or shedding of the hoof takes place, in

two

two or three days. If this misfortune happens to all four feet at once, the animal must be immediately consigned to the slaughtering house ; we must not expect the reproduction of a new hoof, except when the fall of the hoof takes places in one foot only ; and it often happens, that foundering attacks the foot that has been obliged to support the whole weight of the body for a long while. The part reproduced is always more or less feeble and deformed, and the horse is only fit for the purposes of husbandry.

When the separation of the hoof does not take place, it becomes totally deformed ; the toe grows long and bends upwards ; the surface of it is covered with irregularities called circles, or the sole is pushed outwards by the coffin bone, which draws nearer to the perpendicular line, by detaching itself from the interior surface of the hoof; consequently, the inferior surface of the foot becomes convex, and this conformation takes the name of crescent. In this state the horse is obliged to bear entirely on the heels and frog, and the leg in moving describes a semi-circle mi-circle from within outwards, which in French is called swimming.

When the distemper has been less violent than in the preceding case, although it does not occasion the deformity of the feet, yet the horse treads with more or less difficulty, especially at coming out of the stable. The play of the joint being confined, the leg moves with difficulty, and it is then said, though improperly, that the horse is stiff in his shoulders. When indeed the obstacle to motion is in the inferior articulations, bathing them in warm mineral water, or in the mud of those waters, has often produced good effects.

LECTURE

LECTURE VI.

Containing a Description of the Case, commonly known under the Denomination of a Strain in the Back-sinews, and its Rupture; the Fracture of the Bone of the Coronet, the Navicular Bone, the Bone of the Foot, &c.

ALL authors who have written on the accidents incident to the legs of horses, mention the extension of the tendons of the extensor muscles of the foot, vulgarly called, *a strain in the back-sinews*; they describe the causes after their own manner, and prescribe the remedies which they think best adapted for the cure. I am sorry to differ in opinion from them; but I am convinced, that no such accident can ever take place, and that

A a

they

they are deceived by the erroneous ideas they form of the mechanism of the organs of motion, particularly of the legs.

Let us endeavour to explain what we here advance: and in the first place we shall lay down, that tendons are incapable of extension: in the next place, that they are not intended to maintain the bony parts in their places, which function belongs to the ligaments; and when the muscles at all contribute to that effect, the tendons, which are their appendages, are passively employed. This requires a further explanation: let us take the muscles of the foot for an example.

Nature, ever wise and economical in her productions, has provided the muscles with a certain bulk and strength, sufficient to move the parts to which they are affixed; and by this means has proportioned the power to the resistance ; at the same time preserving a light and elegant form, which the too great bulk of the muscles, or their multiplicity, would infallibly have prevented.

The conversion of fleshy fibres into tendinous, renders their insertion in the substance of the bone more solid; the fleshy part possessing a power of motion equal to the natural resistance, it would have been unnecessary for the tendon to possess the same faculty; it is therefore employed, on the contrary, as a fixed point for the action of the muscular fibres.

If we were to grant a slight degree of elasticity in the tendinous fibres, this would add nothing to the possibility of extension in the tendon; because, an effort capable of destroying the natural degree of extension and flexion of the articulated parts, would lacerate the muscular fibres, before the tendinous fibres would receive the smallest injury; therefore the tendon is incapable of distention. This part may, indeed, be broken, but it is by an effort very different from that which we have just supposed, and which shall be explained in treating of the rupture of tendons. If the tendons were employed in maintaining the bones in their places, the muscular fibres would be constantly distended, or violently

contracted

contracted.   In either case the action of the parts would be checked.   The principal function of the muscles and tendons, therefore, consists in giving motion to the parts, and not in supporting them.   I have already said that the ligaments alone are employed in this last function; the ligaments would therefore be lacerated by any effort whatever, before the tendons would feel the least effect; which proves, that these last parts are not exposed to the extensions which are daily complained of.

Let us suggest an experiment, which will elucidate all we have advanced: take the fore leg of a horse, dissect the flexor muscles of the foot, and also the suspensor ligament of the pastern; afterwards, place the leg in its natural position, that is to say, perpendicularly; steady the articulation of the knee to prevent its flexion, and lay on the superior part of it a considerable weight, that shall exceed that which it naturally supports; afterwards, cut transversely the tendons of the flexor muscles, or the *back-sinews*, and you will find that the suspensor ligament

ligament alone is sufficient to keep the articulation of the pastern in its place; observe that the whole weight of the body falls on this part, since all the parts beneath it, as the pastern, coronet, and foot, are removed from the perpendicular, by describing an oblique line, which forms with the shank-bone, an angle of, at least, 25 degrees. If, on the contrary, you cut the suspensor ligament, you will see the articulation in question fall almost to the ground, and the muscles distended to such a degree, as to make it impossible for them to contract themselves, or even to oppose any resistance in this violent state, should the case happen in a living subject. It will certainly be objected, that operations made on dead bodies do not always produce the same result which is observed in living animals; but here the question is only of a purely mechanical operation, which may be attempted without any doubt of success. I shall not pretend to deny the slight degree of contraction which the extensor muscles exert, in order to keep the leg strait when standing; but this action is reduced almost to nothing, when the limb itself is placed in a perpendicular position.

What then is the cause of those swellings which we so frequently observe along the tendons or sinews of the leg, after violent galloping, or after any effort whatever, commonly called *strains?* this is the question that we are now about to investigate. I do not speak here of those swellings which are the result of long continued exercise, or long rest, or which depend upon internal causes; but of those only which are occasioned by some violent effort, as in the case when a horse treads on an irregular surface, or when he leaps too suddenly, without being duly prepared; or executes the leap badly; in either case, the ligaments which determine the extent of the flexion and extension of the parts, are distended and strained, in proportion to the power acting on them at the instant of the exertion, in consequence of their want of elasticity. It is also on this account, that the pain occasioned thereby is great, and of long duration. It is this sharp pain, which, irritating the neighbouring parts, inflames them, and causes the blood and humours to lodge there; but the ligaments themselves, being composed of an extremely hard texture,

which

which receives scarcely any kind of vessels, are not liable to swelling. The increase of bulk of the leg therefore, is nothing more than a symptom of the complaint, and not the complaint itself, as has been too commonly supposed. The seat of the affection is still less in the tendons, since I have made it clear that the rupture of the muscles must take place before the tendons can be at all affected, in case of a strain.

I am already persuaded, that many will find the mechanical and anatomical explanations given here, difficult to be understood; but I must acquaint my readers in general, that I do not write for those who think they are masters of the subject, because such persons do not stand in need of my instructions; but for those only who are either already initiated in the science, or who are desirous of obtaining information; to the former these explanations will not be obscure, and to the latter, a very little attention and assiduity will render them familiar.

Let

Let us now return to our object, and endeavour to establish conviction on all we have said. If, for example, we were to dissect the leg of a horse, labouring under a *strain in the back-sinews*, according to the vulgar notion, we should discover no affection in the substance of the tendinous parts, which, on the contrary, would appear in their natural state; but if the surrounding parts were examined, we should observe, according to the duration of the disease, a relaxation in the sheaths of the tendons, or in the capsulary ligament of the articulation; or, in short, in the whole vascular system.

If the ailment is of long standing, and nature has exhausted all her resources in endeavouring to discuss the stagnated humours without being able to succeed completely, a small hard swelling will appear in the sheaths of the tendons, sometimes two, and even three, which are called *ganglions*; whose situation near the tendons is sufficient to make the horse walk lame for the remainder of his life. These *ganglions* are often the result of a bad cure; particu-

larly

larly when powerful astringents have been employed too early, having previously neglected the use of emollients. For instance, an unshod horse, who, in a quick pace, such as a gallop, sets his toe upon a stone, may be violently strained, because in this false step, or wrong position of the foot, the articulations of the bone of the foot, the pastern, and coronet, are stretched in their flexion; but the strain will become more dangerous, if the foot is shod with a shoe with very thick heels, and if the sole and frog are too much pared away; because, these parts being too far distant from the ground, and the frog being, as I have often had occasion to say, intended to support a part of the weight of the body, it is thereby rendered incapable of affording a purchase to the articulations. In this case the effort is communicated to the bone of the foot, or coffin bone, which presses upon the fleshy sole; and the pressure upon this part is often so violent, as to make it the seat of the disease. This is so true, that frequently a cure can only be obtained by the operation of unsoling.

B b

The

The principles here laid down, might be supported by a variety of observations on the mechanism of the animal machine; but this would lead me too far from my purpose. Those anatomists who may peruse this discourse, will be more capable of developing and extending the imperfect ideas, which I have ventured to advance on a case, which I believe has been hitherto badly described, and as badly treated. I proceed now to the symptoms which caracterise it. These symptoms are, the swelling which appears between the knee and pastern, and extends even to the heels; the tension, heat, and pain of the part, which occasions the horse to walk more or less lame.

It must be observed, that these symptoms are common to other cases; such as a nail driven into the quick, or a blow on the tendon; they may be equally the effect of long exercise, or an accumulation of humours, in the case of an acute disease. It is therefore necessary to examine with great caution and reflexion, before we give a decided opinion on the nature and cause of the complaint. But if a horse,

                                        perfectly

perfectly free in his limbs, is suddenly attacked with a lameness, attended with swelling on the part just mentioned, and if this should happen after hard running, a leap, a fall, or a slip, without any blow, contusion, or wound in the tendon, we may then suspect the existence of a strain in the ligaments, and in the sheaths of the tendons. But, as I have already observed that in this case the fleshy fibres would participate in the effect of this extension, we should not neglect to feel the extensor muscle of the foot, which is situated at the hinder part of the arm; in order to discover whether the animal experiences any pain in that part. When the disease is ascertained, there remains only to prescribe proper remedies, for the affected parts.

Astringents are most commonly the remedies employed to produce a revulsion of the humour. These succeed, if the accident is not violent, and if they are employed; but, if two or three days are allowed to elapse after the accident, before they are applied, they, on the contrary, fix the humour in the part and

coagulate

coagulate it; constrict the vessels, check the circulation, and at length occasion indurations, the effect of the concretion of the fluids.

As it would be in vain to interrogate our brute-patients on their situation, and as grooms, through design or ignorance, are more or less apt to deceive us, we ought always to suspect the disease to be of some standing, and consequently should employ emollient substances, as the properest to begin the cure with, in the following manner.

For this purpose, take mallows, marsh-mallows, pellitory of the wall, of each one handful, boil them for three quarters of an hour, in common water, chop them fine for a poultice, which is to be applied to the leg, from the knee down to the foot, and which is to be moistened every three hours with some of the emollient decoction. The following ingredients will answer the same purpose, take crumb of bread, boil it in cow's milk, to which add one drachm of saffron,

saffron, or barley meal, mixed with a sufficient quantity of the emollient decoction, made of mallows, &c. or, for want of these ingredients, use warm water, by way of bath, or fomentation; it is the most powerful relaxant, in human as well as in veterinary medicine. If in eight or ten days the pain is not lessened, it will be necessary immediately to unsole the foot; because, it will be a proof of the pressure of the bone of the foot upon the fleshy sole, a pressure which occurs oftener than is supposed, in consequence of the strain treated of in this lecture.

If, notwithstanding the treatment here recommended, the swelling should not be entirely dissipated, in about a month, or more, and if there should remain certain hard substances, called *ganglions*, seated in the sheaths of the tendons, we must determine on the operation of firing, as the most powerful resolvent. This operation, to which I am no great friend, often produces good effects when not applied too late; that is to say, when applied before the humour becomes concreted, and the tumour insensible,

and

and hard, in the latter circumstances, the effect of firing goes no further, than to extract what little fluid may remain in the affected part, by the in-flammation and suppuration it creates; it increases the hardness, and for ever prevents its discussion. Experience having shewn, that remaining a long time in the stable is hurtful to the diseased part after the operation of firing, it will be requisite to exercise the horse daily, in order to promote the cure.

In the beginning of this lecture, I said, that ten-dons are not capable of extension, and at the same time, I allowed the possibility of their rupture: these assertions may appear contradictory to those who are not versed in the knowledge of anatomy, nor acquainted with the laws of mechanics; it is ne-vertheless easy to conceive, that a sudden degree of force, suddenly exerted on a fixed point of an ex-tended rope, is capable of breaking it at that point, though the opposite point be not in the least de-ranged; and that the same degree of force, em-ployed successively on all the other points of the
                                                          rope,

rope, will not even be able to stretch it. Any foreign power whatever, acting on the cords of an animated machine, produces the same effects. For instance, if a horse sets his feet badly on the ground,
or places his leg in a false direction, at the instant he
is obliged to make a violent effort, directing all his
force on the lower insertion of the tendon, this latter part may be suddenly broken, or snapped, and
separated from the bone, while the rest of the tendon, and even the muscle, will have experienced no
sensible degree of extension.

However, this accident is easily to be known from
the following symptoms: First. When the animal
attempts to walk, he is able to stretch out his foot to
carry it forward, but he cannot possibly bend it backward; because, the flexor muscles having lost their
fixed point, can no longer act. Secondly, For this
same reason, when the tendon is examined, it is
found in a state of slackness, from the knee down to
the pastern, instead of being more or less tight, as is
the case when no rupture has taken place. Thirdly,

The

The horse appears to feel an acute pain when the fingers are inserted between the heels.   Fourthly, A swelling is soon perceived in this part, which indicates a collection of humours; but it is of the utmost importance, not to wait for the appearance of this last symptom; because the collected matter is capable of making great havock, particularly in the articulation of the foot; which, when once open, renders the case absolutely incurable, and finally destroys the animal.   To prevent this accident, which of all others is the worst and last, the foot must be immediately unsoled, an opening made in the fleshy frog sufficient to bring the extremity of the tendon to view, and upon which some proper relaxing ointment may be laid, such as the simple digestive, the use of which must be continued until a portion of the tendon falls off in the manner of an exfoliation; without which, a cure can never be obtained.   The wound is afterwards to be dressed with spirituous applications, as the tincture of myrrh, of aloes, and the spirit of turpentine; but, as it is impossible to get hold of, and at the same time to retain the extremity

tremity of the tendon in the place of its original insertion, that is to say, on the bone of the foot, we can entertain no hopes of a perfect cure. The best we can expect is, that the tendon may adhere and unite itself to the bone of the coronet, which however confuses the mechanism of the foot. We accordingly find, that almost all horses that have been treated for a similar accident, remain for the most part lame during the remainder of their lives; nevertheless, in this state, some horses may still be of use.

The bone of the foot, or coffin bone, is also liable to be fractured; this rare accident occasions a very painful lameness. The causes producing it are nearly the same as those which occasion the rupture of the tendon; that is to say, the wrong position of the foot, at the instant the horse exerts his strength, either simply to move forward, or to carry or draw a heavy weight. In this case the tendon is snapped from the bone, or the bone of the foot is fractured; which of these is determined by the accu-

c c   mulation

mulation or direction of the force on one or the other of these parts. It must be owned that the fracture in question is not easily discovered; the only symptom to make us suspect its existence is, the swelling of the coronet, and the pain which the horse feels when that part is pressed. But, before determining this point, we must enter into a scrupulous examination of all the parts of the limb. If, however, we suppose the disease in question really to exist, the method of cure is extremely simple; it consists chiefly in unsoling the foot, in order to prevent the bad effects of inflammation, by giving vent to the humours, which would otherwise produce great havock within the hoof; and in keeping the animal perfectly still and quiet; and, as the fractured bone is surrounded and confined by solid parts, and its motion, besides, being extremely limited, nature will easily effect a re-union. At the expiration of three months, the horse may be sent to grass for a short time; and, if circumstances will permit, should be moderately exercised upon soft ground, by which means a more perfect cure will be effected.

Being

Being confined in these lectures to the consideration of the foot alone, I cannot, without departing
from my plan, speak of the diseases incident to the ad-
jacent parts; nevertheless, the bone of the articulation being contained within the hoof, and lying con-
tiguous to the coronet bone; I cannot terminate
this work without saying a few words on the fracture of these two latter bones. It cannot be denied,
from their situation, that they support the whole
weight of the body, even in an oblique direction;
that in every motion of the animal, this weight must
be equally distributed, on every point of the articulated surfaces; and that, consequently, any action
which causes an unequal distribution of that weight,
throwing it suddenly on a single point, incapable of
sustaining it, undoubtedly fractures the bone. This
accident is not easily discovered in the bone of the
foot, but may be often ascertained in the coronet,
when the swelling is not great, by pressing the fractured pieces together, by which means a sensible degree of friction is produced. The reduction of these
fractures is not in the power of art. It would be

useless

useless to attempt the application of a bandage; and as it is impossible to make a horse keep his leg up horizontally, as upon a chair, there is no other method than to abandon the cure to the agency of nature. The horse must be kept, if possible, in a perfect state of rest; at the same time anodyne poultices should be employed to calm the pain, the violence of which is able to create a fever, and even to produce a suppuration in the affected parts.

Having hitherto omitted to mention an accident that frequently occurs, called a prick of the foot in shoeing, I shall terminate this lecture with a few words on this subject.

It may happen to the most skilful farrier, to prick a horse in shoeing, either by a motion of the horse, while the nail is driving; or, when the nail takes a wrong direction from the horny substance being too hard; in either of which cases, the point not being able to penetrate the wall, makes its way into the parts which offer the least resistance.

Sometimes

Sometimes the blade of the nail splits in two, one part of which is forced outwardly, while the other penetrates within. It also happens sometimes, that the nail meets, in driving, with a remnant of an old nail, which turns it out of its direction, and forces it into the quick : this latter part though not pricked, may be compressed by a weak nail bent inwardly. In all these cases, if the nail is drawn immediately, no bad consequence follows; even if blood should appear at the orifice, it will require no operation, nor the application of any remedy: but if the nail should remain some days in the foot, an inflammation, and frequently a suppuration takes place in the affected part. In this case, having ascertained exactly the seat of the wound, an opening must be made between the wall and the sole, deep enough to reach the bottom of the wound, and to bring to view the inflamed and suppurated parts, and a free issue given to the matter. The wound is afterwards to be dressed with spirituous applications, such as the spirits of turpentine, tincture of myrrh, aloes, &c.

If

If the prick is of long standing, if the pus or matter, has not only affected the foliated substance, the fleshy sole, the bone of the foot, but which sometimes happens, has even penetrated to the coronet, not only an incision is to be made in the upper and lower part, but suppuratives also, such as the simple digestive mixed with basilicum, must be applied in order to facilitate its issue.   If the pus should have affected the cartilage, the operation for a simple quitter must be immediately performed, which consists in separating the portions of the cartilage, rendered carious by the pus.

If the horny sole seems partly separated from the fleshy sole, we must determine to unsole the foot, persuaded, that the cure is infinitely more certain, and more speedy, when all the contaminated parts are exposed to view, than when the matter is permitted to burrow and form other sinuses.   It would be useless to enter into a fresh detail, to explain the treatment of the wound.   It is sufficient to say, that the bony, cartilaginous, tendinous or aponeurotic parts,
                                                                    are

are to be dressed with spirituous applications; fleshy parts, with the simple digestive at first, and afterwards with spirituous, and the cure terminated by dissicatives.

Among the number of shoes mentioned in the course of this work, there are two of which I have given only the names, but which, on account of their utility, deserve particular attention; these are the scate shoes: See plate the second, No. 7, and 8.

Let us suppose a case in which they are to be used. In a horse, for instance, labouring under a long lameness, the continual pain which he feels in the extremity of the limb, constantly obliges him to throw all the weight of his body on the sound leg, so that the lame leg is always in a state of flexion. The muscles, the tendons, and the ligaments, insensibly lose their action, for want of exercise; the circulation is retarded in every part of the limb; which is thus deprived of the nourishing juice intended for its support; a spontaneous contraction takes place,

in

in the organs of motion, the effect of which is such,
that it often happens, that after curing the disease,
the leg remains strait, the fetlock is carried forwards,
and the horse walks upon the toe.   When this accident is neglected, it will resist all the efforts of nature and art, and the animal remains lame all his
life; and it is easy to foresee it and provide against
it, or to attack it in its origin, by the following method.

When we observe in the leg a propensity to remain in a state of flexion, and that the extension is
not compleated, even when the weight of the body
bears upon it, it must be held in the emollient bath,
three times a day, for the space of two hours each
time; and in the intervals, a poultice of the same
nature, composed of emollient plants, applied to the
fore legs, from the elbows to the feet; and from the
thigh to the foot, in the hind feet; afterwards, the
horse must be shod in the following manner, with
the shoes already mentioned: the end proposed by
using this shoe, is to effect a progressive extension

sion of the muscles of the affected limb, as well as a relaxation of the ligaments, by which means the parts may be brought insensibly to their natural situation.

To obtain this end, the shoe No. 7, must be applied to the foot of the lame leg, which, by its prolongation at the toe, determines the fetlock backwards, and obliges the horse to bear more particularly on his heels. Afterwards, apply the shoe No. 8, to the foot of the sound leg, which is raised in a small degree, by means of the three caulkings of the shoe in question. ' Consequently, if the horse endeavours to throw the weight of the body on this leg, he is obliged to extend it; in this case, the diseased leg becomes too short; but, as the horse cannot remain a long time in this position, he mechanically directs the weight of his body to the diseased leg, and the moment this leg reaches the ground, the other must of necessity bend itself.

It is easy to conceive, by this double operation, that the extensor muscles re-assume progressively

D d

their

their functions, and that the flexor muscles are so far extended, as to cause the parts of the leg to return to their natural direction and situation.

The too frequent use of blisters, in the accident here considered, ought to be rejected, as well as that of firing, which cannot but increase the evil, and even render it incurable.

Here I terminate these lectures, which I offer only as elements of the art of shoeing, and of the accidents and diseases incident to the foot: there now remains nothing more than for me to endeavour to animate the pupils, to possess themselves of the principles here laid down, and to endeavour, in the course of their practice, to super-add new ones; and I shall esteem it a real reward of my labours, if any one among them should go beyond me in the career in which I am engaged.

F I N I S.

GENERAL OBSERVATIONS

ON THE ART OF

VETERINARY MEDICINE.

I.

DISEASE is the lot of all organized bodies; man, brutes, and even plants, are subject to it.

It is that deviation from health, which, in a greater or lesser degree, disorders the frame and spirits, yielding either to some critical effort of Nature or of Art, or, by its unremitting resistence, destroying the fabric by producing death.

Health

II.

Health then being the regular discharge of all
the functions of the body, and of the faculty of
freely and perfectly exercising them; and death,
on the other hand, being the entire extinction of
that faculty, and a total cessation of those functions; we can form no other conception and con-
clusion respecting the interval between the derangement, either in the general frame, or in some
of its parts, which more or less disturbs the harmony of its motions, than what constitutes precisely that which is called and known by the
general name of disease.

III.

To prevent, as much as in us lies, the origin
of those disorders in animals, which do not arise
from

from accident, infection, or contagion; by attaining to a knowledge of that kind of food and treatment which is conducive to health, and by carefully avoiding to administer that which may be noxious and prejudicial to it; to mitigate the violence of those disorders which reduce the value of animals, without at the same time rendering them altogether useless, and also to endeavour to subdue and eradicate others by every method which the knowledge of things suitable to each disorder can suggest, is the object of the veterinary art.

IV.

The object of this art is therefore not only congenial with that of human medicine; but the very same paths which lead to the knowledge of the diseases of man, lead equally to the knowledge of those of brutes. An accurate examination of the interior parts of their bodies, a studious survey of the arrangement, structure,

form,

form, connection, use, and relation of these parts, and of the laws by which they are intended to act, as also of the nature and properties of the various foods, and other agents, which the earth so liberally provides for their support and cure ; these form, in a great measure, the sound and sure foundations of all medical science, whatever living individual animal is the subject of our consideration.

V.

It is evident therefore, that veterinary medicine requires a degree of knowledge of no less extent than that which is exercised upon the human body ; and we may venture to assert, without infringing the respect due to the latter, that the former is in very many instances obliged to engage in more minute researches, and in longer and more laborious investigation ; it is not, like human medicine, limited to the study of one spe-

cies

cies only, it commprehends the care of every
kind of useful animal; the preservation of which
forms its peculiar province; it is indeed true,
that researches multiplied in the examination of
different subjects, whose respective mechanisms
all conspire to produce nearly the same effects,
afford great advantages to the veterinary physician, by enabling him, from comparison, to
throw additional light on many subjects.

VI.

If, pursuing this fascinating track of investigation, we wish to avoid falling into error, we must
studiously guard against the illusion of self-con-
ceit, and of that presumption which seems ever to
take delight in concealing from our reason the
impassable line Nature has drawn between herself
and us, by not hastily deducing as conclusive,
from the first data we may acquire, consequnces
which experience may afterwards demonstrate to

have

have been too hastily drawn : In rejecting all speculative inference and theory, concerning the structure and functions of the different parts, however apparently well founded ; in not sub-mitting our judgment to mere authority ; in be-coming the slave of no opinion ; in discarding every prejudice ; in admitting for truth that only which has been faithfully deduced from a steady, constant, and unprejudiced observation. In a word, by yielding only to facts, and being guided by their immediate consequences ; which alone will effectually guard us against the dogmas of system, the monument equally of the erring pride and weakness of the human mind, which, though it may impose for a while, will sooner or later, by experiment and reason, be done away.

VII.

Principles thus confirmed to us by practice, and from which no consequences are attempted

to

to be drawn, but such as naturally flow from thence, can never mislead us. An accurate and quick eye, a ready and happy penetration, a free and sound judgment, are qualities rarely concentred in one person, though indispensable in order to become eminent in the art of physic or of surgery : how exquisite must be the discernment and touch, to judge of and determine with some degree of certainty the existence of particular diseases, their causes and kind, their seat, state, and progress ; to draw, by comparing different appearances, the proper inference ; and by analogy, amongst a multitude of symptoms, resulting from a variety of constitutions and habits, to anticipate the issue; to attain to the means wherewith to subdue it, by the particular circumstances of the subject at-tacked ; and lastly, to suspend or abate our ef-forts when we have arrived at that point beyond which we cannot proceed without being involved in risk and uncertainty !

VIII.

VIII.

Nor is less judgment required in our attention to every step of Nature in this oppressed situation, in order to discover the course and method she designs to adopt for relief; or, if she fails in her indication, to urge her, by a seasonable interference, to discover it; which if happily attained, to second by every skilful aid the efforts she makes for such relief; but if her indications are of an unpropitious nature, to moderate, and endeavour to controul, those which are tumultuous and acute, whilst we assist and support such as are weak and insufficient; and thus by conforming with unwearied attention and judgment to her designs, to arrive at the most gratifying situation of human art, the being able to subdue and extinguish those causes and things which are injurious and destructive, or at least to provide against the evil consequences they might occasion

casion if not thus treated. Thus led on by caution and skill, we shall not interfere with what is entirely dependent on Nature; but confine ourselves scrupulously within the limits of art, so far as relates to her indications and to her relief.

IX.

No one therefore can be so absurd to imagine, that it is possible without preparatory study, and a due course of investigation and experimental knowledge, to attain to the great ends before mentioned. Without these acquirements, the art of medicine is an hypothesis, which neither natural endowment, or mere instinct can sanction; and of course it is liable to such perpetual error, as must lead to consequences the most dangerous. On the other hand, we are not to place implicit confidence in study alone, or to give intire credit to any decision proceeding from this single source, when the grand question of life and health is con-

c   cerned

cerned : so also the man who relies upon practice alone (being destitute of the fundamental principles of study and investigation) will meet with so many obstructions and mortifications in the exercise of his profession, that he will lament his want of those acquirements, which are the result of properly blending study and investigation with practice.

X.

It is then from a due combination of study, investigation, and practice, that we can attain to the solid effects and advantages of enlightened and successful science : united and directed by skill and sound judgment, they mutually support and correct each other ; they embrace all that is beneficial, salutary, and consolatory to afflicted Nature.

XI.

XI.

Unhappily for veterinary medicine, it is at present lamentably deficient in all these acquirements; yet having access to the great mine of knowledge, derived from those philosophers and original investigators, of the organization and texture of the various animals subjected to their researches, either when devoted to public sacrifice, or to the more painful, yet useful discovery, by living subjects, not only tracing in that organization and texture, but also from whence the great and essential causes of life and death : (investigations which have proved of the greatest general benefit :) the veterinarian may find not only substantial information, but be induced to open the wonderful page of modern discovery so far as relates to the human structure. These great lights, if zealously followed, will lead us on, and become the surest pledges of a real progress and improvement

C 2   provement

provement in the art. But, in pursuing our researches, we must use every caution, that we do not graft upon analogy what may be productive of error : to guard against which, we should have recourse to investigation and experiment faithfully pursued ; to comparison and inference accurately made and cautiously deduced.

XII.

Having proceeded in my general observations so far as they relate to the fundamental principles of the art, I shall now proceed to elucidate and confirm the necessity of a strict adherence to these principles, by a short view of the present state of veterinary knowledge and practice in what is called farriery, and cow-doctoring, &c. in Great Britain, from the information I have been able to attain respecting the mode and manner thereof.

As very many of the hereditary dispositions of a number of animals of different kinds, collected for the purposes of agriculture, manufacture, and commerce, are, by being continually dispersed into counties they were not bred in, so altered, that it is not possible for any local data to be formed as to those diseases which seem to prevail, and to belong to one county, and not to another: So neither can we say, with certainty, from whence the superior strength, or inferior weakness; or why the morbific cause of disorders, which appear to be almost hereditary in one part of the kingdom, do not shew one similar symptom in another: Or why the county of Suffolk should produce a short, close-made, strong, under-sized breed of horses, when that of the mid-land counties nearly doubles the size of the Suffolk horses: Or why the counties of York and Durham should excel the rest for racers, hunters, and hacks: Neither are we better informed of the manner of breeding which they have hitherto practised; the quantity and quality of food, or of water, to which they have been accustomed; nor, with precision, the specific kind

of

of labour to which they have been put ; or of the hereditary and prevalent disorders to which the animals of the different counties are most sub-ject : much less has there been any regular re-cord of the application and effect of medicine for their relief, so that we might be better able to investigate, and generally assist the veterinary practice.   All at this moment appears obscured or bewildered by the ill-placed confidence of the owners of cattle upon the blacksmith of the parish ; upon illiterate and conceited grooms, stupid and listless shepherds ; or upon a set of men infinitely more dangerous than all the rest, who, arrogating to themselves the style of doctors, ride about from town to town distributing their nostrums, compounded of the refuse and vapid scraps of druggists shops, to the destruction of thousands, whose varied disorders they treat alike, neither consulting nature or art for the cause or the effect.

Miserable animal ! bereft of speech, thou can'st not complain, when to the disease with which

thou art afflicted, excruciating torments are super-
added, by the ignorant efforts of such men who,
at first sight, and without any investigation to lead
them to the source of thy disorder, pronounce a
hackneyed, common-placed opinion on thy case,
and then proceed, with all expedition, to open
thy veins, lascerate thy flesh, cauterize thy sinews,
and drench thy stomach with drugs, adverse in
general to the cure they engage to perform.

Opposed to this barbarian and noxious practice, let us turn our eye to that of the veterinary
physician and surgeon. We shall not find him
occupying the attention of his auditors with ac-
counts of miraculous cures he never performed ;
or, under the mask of sullen arrogance, endeavouring to attract confidence : we shall not
see him armed at all points with fleams,
rowelling-knives, and cauterizing-irons, to rack
and torment his suffering patients ; or with
drenches and balls, to obstruct the efforts of
Nature. We shall see him, with a cautious eye,
and

and tender hand, surveying and examining, with discretion and judgment, into the case before him; and, as far as he can attain information from those who bring the animal to him, we shall find him an anxious and patient enquirer : proceeding to explore all the external signs, and to observe, with great minuteness, every symptom which presents itself ; and, if he finds them so complicated he cannot proceed with certainty to give an opinion, he will wait till some new, or more distinct appearances come to his assistance. If, however, these signs should not shew themselves to a given effect, he will then apply to the only resource left him, that of compelling Nature to develope herself, or, at least, to shew some indications. This he accomplishes by stimulating her, through the means of medicinal aid, administered in proper quantities, which, by encreasing more or less sensibly, the disease, produces some discovery of its tendency.

But if the case proves intricate and obstinate, accompanied by a vicious turn of temper in the

animal, far from being discouraged, it only encreases his ardour, and stimulates his zeal. He
summonses every power, and tries every method,
to put in practice those principles of science,
and of art, he possesses, to meet all the dificul-
ties of the case. If, however, after these efforts,
he finds he cannot ascend to first causes, he
then guides himself by the most favourable indications he can attain; and he is sometimes
so fortunate, by following half symptoms only,
to overcome some of the most obstinate cases,
though he could not reach the immediate source
of the disease.

This close attention, and method of treatment,
is extremely necessary, nay, indispensable in
most cases of epizootic contagion; more especially when it proceeds from the temperature
and condition of the air, or from the vitiated
quality of the grass, and other herbs on which
cattle feed.

D   Always

Always judicious in the choice of his medical apparatus and in the administering of drugs, he avoids the discordant medley, and pernicious recipes and treatment too frequently laid down in farriers' books ; well knowing, that both human and veterinary science would soon fall into error, if the same drug, which acts differently upon different habits, was to be administered alike to all : that therefore, according to local circumstances, habit, temper, and symptom, must be his mode of prescribing the remedy to the disease.　For want of this discernment and circumspection, the most salutary medicines have frequently proved pernicious.　Add to this the dreadful effects often produced by the unskilful speculatist's tampering with the medicinal properties of drugs, the inherent qualities of which he is totally ignorant of. At the beginning of a disease, the veterinary physician prudently prescribes those medicines only which are mild in their effects, in order to gain a more clear knowledge of the constitution of his patient, and also that he may not occasion any

unfavour-

unfavourable turn or alteration in the disease it-self; thus sparing the habit of the sufferer, he obtains more solid advantages than by sudden, violent efforts: He is also governed, in some measure, by the temperature and state of the air. He prescribes active medicines for animals whose muscular texture is feeble and unelastic, and whose juices are not sufficiently fluid: He pursues a different treatment to those whose elasticity and fluids are more susceptible of irritation; varying his efforts as the necessity of each case requires: He never provokes evacuations till he has allowed Nature sufficient time for providing the proper matter to be evacuated, and that the passages are in an open and free state for such an effort: He guards against their taking place through irregular or improper channels; and that the operation of one should not interfere with those it may be thought right to promote at the same time in another part of the body. He is particularly attentive to the critical evacuations, or efforts which Nature makes, at

some

some stages of a disease; and if she appears too languid, or feeble, to perfect them, he co-operates with her, by every aid in his power. He knows how to distinguish acute from chronic; and to adopt the proper mode of treating each of these diseases: His skill assists him to remove or divert, from the *vitals* to the less-essential parts, those disorders which would soon prove fatal to *them*, but not so to the other: And he adds, a proper regimen, rigorously adhered to, in aid of his medicinal efforts; debarring the animal from all solid food, wherever it may, from the state of the disease, become corrupted by the fluids which contribute to a wholesome digestion, being unable to perform this salutary office. Thus accomplished in science and in art, if he can say that a part of his knowledge was obtained in that universal school an hospital, he feels himself perfectly conscious in his abilities: If to these acquirements he adds those of liberality and honour, he makes the *utile dulcis*, the pleasure of being useful, precede every sentiment of reward.

It

It would not be lost time, if the student was to attain to an use and readiness in stenography, or short-hand writing: this would enable him to store up much information, and to correct many errors in practice, by noting the minutiæ, as well as the more striking circumstances, that have attended his successes, or his failures; he would be in possession of every word that has been pronounced, and of every elucidation that has confirmed the observation; it would also enable him to mark with more precision his own inferences and opinions.

_AN

ESSAY ON THE GREASE,

OR

WATERY SORES IN THE LEGS OF HORSES.*

> " I wish that every one would only write
> what he knows, and as much as he knows."
>
> MONTAIGNE.

I.

THE grease is in general a cutaneous chronic disease, sometimes inflammatory, sometimes infectious; and I have known it contageous: it invades the legs of horses, asses, and mules; but seldom attacks those of the ruminating species.

II.

* This Essay obtained the prize given by the Royal Society of Medicine; it being the best treatise produced on the subject that year. Vide page 10th of the Memoirs.

II.

It discovers itself by an obstruction either in the coronet, in the pastern, or in the fetlock joint, attended with pain more or less violent. These first symptoms compel the animal frequently to raise the affected limb suddenly, as though touched with something sharp or rough. If these irritations are not mitigated in this stage of the disease, they soon encrease, and produce a grey or green fœtid sanies, which, oozing through the skin, excoriates wherever it is suffered to lodge, and adds not only to the inflammation, but irritation of the part affected. In this second stage of the disease, the inflammation and obstruction generally rises upwards, spreading itself sometimes as high as the knee or hock; the animal then becomes lame; and if put to work, from the part affected oozes a thin, ichorous matter, tinged with blood; the running humour

assumes

assumes soon after a spissitude, and becomes unctuous and greasy to the touch. If the disease affects the coronet, it makes the horn of the hoof grow, rendering it at the same time soft and spongy, sometimes unsoldering and separating the hoof from the crown, and but too often destroying the frog of the foot : the stubbed hair, called the bristle, falls off, shewing the skin sometimes of a dead white, at other times of a livid colour, and oedematocis full of little bladders, many of which, becoming confluent, soon form ulcers, in part covered with granulated flesh, resembling a fungus, called, by some, warts, grapes, proud-flesh, &c. others, being more confluent, resemble the outward coat of a pine-apple, or a large piece of a honey-comb; however, in my opinion, if this disease appear on the coronet, it is better denominated the crown scab; on the heels, an ulcerated frog; upon the fore part of the pastern joint, and about the hoof, a quitter; along the tendons, rat-tails; and mallenders and sallenders, when on the joints of the knees and hocks.

E These

These ulcers often allure, during the summer and autumn, that species of fly which delights to lay its eggs upon unsound or corrupted flesh ; these soon assuming the form of maggots, they add a stimulus to the disease, and by making deep chaps, exuding a purulent, discoloured sanies, attended by a steeming vapour of so volatile and acrimonious a quality, that, by its itching, the animal is tormented nearly to madness : it corrodes and destroys the teguments, over which it runs as powerfully as the most active and strong caustic.   In this stage of the disease, it is very difficult to cure hurts from bad shoeing ; and wounds, or punctures, by cuts, or nails perforating the foot ; over-reach cuts, or a sandcrack.   Lastly, the skin gradually extends by the encrease of these sanious humours ; the discharge becomes so abundant, that every hair left upon it serves to convey, in large and successive drops, a brown or blueish liquor, whose intolerable stench pollutes the circumambient air, rendering the road, pasture, or stable, not only

offensive,

offensive, but, in the confined state of the latter, actually noxious : this stench is as characteristic of the grease in its last stage, as the one which attends the farcy marks its fatal ravages and period. The leg now becomes an inflated, cumbrous mass of disease; and its motion is limping, attended with great and inflexible stiffness from the anchilosis which seems to take place in the joints; the bone spavin comes on, and the limb nearest that which is thus affected, at times partakes in some measure of the disease; the animal wastes away; and, though the appetite may yet remain, he falls into an athrophy, and is long useless before he is worn out or dies of the disease.

I have observed that the hinder limbs are more frequently affected with this disorder than the anterior; and that though the foreging description of it embraces the general course of its progress and symptoms, yet the veterinarian must expect to encounter many appearances which materially differ, as the constitution, air, food,

work,

work, and exercise, of the subject attacked differ. However, one data, I conceive, will hold good, that this disease cannot be deemed acute, but chronic; and also never reaches its last stage before the term of three months, seldom before nine; and that sometimes it holds its dread career much longer.

III.

Such is the progress of this loathsome disease, generally speaking, when, under the accumulated weight of neglect or unskilful treatment, nature has been perverted and distressed, and her efforts for relief baffled, either by the indolence of the owner, or the more slovenly and injudicious attempts of the empirical blacksmith, called a farrier; and as the latter but too often oppose this disease by violent applications, such as astringents desiccatives, and sometimes with oily substances, by which they clog and choke

up

up the pores, they bring on lameness, dry spavins, foundering, excrescences, tumours, nodes in different parts of the body, and the mange, frequently ending in a foul and confirmed farcy, thus substituting, or rather producing, a greater evil than the one they falsely boast to have cured: from hence also the oedematous swelling of the belly; abcesses in the neck, frequently terminating in a fistula or the pole-evil; a diseased viscera; water in the lower belly, the chest, or the brain; the vertigo; cachexy; peripneumonies; purulent, discoloured urine; violent and inflammatory gripes; abcesses in the viscera of the lower belly and chest; spasms; an affection of the nerves, frequently terminating in convulsions or partial palsies; and those glandular and painful swellings in the lower jaw, the forerunners of that yellow, green, and bloody matter, discharged from the nostrils, which are soon afterwards corroded by deep and virulent ulcers, attended by the anginis, or chronic cough, terminated by fever, the glanders, a marasmus, and death.

Upon dissecting the bodies of horses, &c. which have died in the above diseased state, originating from the ichorous, watery malady, called the grease, I have in general found the whole lean and emaciated; the viscera of the lower belly dry and full of obstructions, more especially the mesentery and pancreas; the liver schirrous and rotten; much hard excrement in the great intestines; the small guts contracted, and frequently containing a number of long, round, whitish worms; the stomach corroded by bots and maw-worms; the lungs diseased, and more or less covered with tubercles filled with a matter resembling soft chalk; the pituitary membrane relaxed, spongy, and covered with yellow, fœtid mucus; the frontal and maxillary sinuses loaded with the same purulent matter. And though these appearances are found in bodies which are destroyed by the farcy, glanders, and other chronic diseases, yet I have uniformly found them in those falling by the grease: the skin of the limb affected has been much thicker than

in

in its healthy state, loose and spongy, perforated in several places ; the cellular texture of it completely choaked up, having the appearance of hogs' skin ; very hard, and adhering to the sheaths of the tendons ; full of a yellow matter, more or or less fœtid and thick ; the blood-vessels varieous, and much dilated ; and, when the disease has been of long standing, I have observed the yellow pus about the skin to be more thick and fœtid, the bony substances to be softened and enlarged, and those of the pastern and coronet affected with exostosis, and the lateral cartilages of the bone of the foot inclining to ossification.

The causes of this dangerous and most noisome disease are either internal or external. The former arise, first, from the nature of the ground whereon the horse, &c. is bred and feeds ; and therefore the Dutch, Flemish, German, and English horses, are more disposed thereto than those who pasture in dry, elevated countries, where this malady is scarce ever to be heard of or found.

found. In general, horses of the abovementioned countries, whose legs are loaded with hair, of a lax and phlegmatic habit of body, who have been bred and brought up in rich and marshy grounds, are more than ordinarily subject to it. I shall now proceed to the other internal causes : the disorders called the strangles, vives, &c. not properly treated and cured, but checked and repelled into the habit ; inflammatory and cutaneous eruptions repelled and checked ; the negligent treatment of brood mares on the reflux of the milk into the blood, upon the death or weaning her colt ; foul and bad nourishment ; excessive labour ; long and injudicious use of sudorifics, and other relaxing and resolving medicines ; super-purgations ; frequent and injudicious bleedings ; obesity ; want of regular exercise ; verminous affections ; the cachexy, dropsy, &c. &c. in a word, whatever tends to destroy, or too much relax, the texture of the solids, or to impoverish or stagnate the fluids.

The

The external causes are as numerous. Whatever suddenly checks perspiration; either by the change of weather from hot to cold; remaining, during the winter nights, in rain or snow; washing the legs in cold well water, while the animal is in a sweat from hard work; confined, narrow, and damp, or wet stables, where the air has not an active and free circulation, too many animals crouded into them; standing in litter saturated with their urine; the indolence, the filthiness, and the want of attention to their bellies, chest, legs, pasterns, coronets, and feet, whereby the gravel, dirt, mud, dust, or sweat, acquired by labour, is suffered to remain and accumulate; want of due currying and dressing; clipping the hair off the legs and pasterns, close to the skin, in the winter, or what is still worse, plucking it out by the roots; excoriations in the pasterns; blows; over-reach cuts; quitters; unskilful blisterings or firings. Grains, with which dray, and other hard-working horses in and about London, are fed, is very productive of this malady;

F

more

more especially where proper treatment and attention, both to cleanliness and medicinal correctors, are not scrupulously adhered to.

This disease is incident to both sexes, and to all ages ; nevertheless, mares and geldings seem to be more subject to it than the entire horse ; but when the latter is diseased, it proves violent and obstinate. The cure is more difficult in youth and old age, than in the middle of the animal's life. I have observed in young horses a greater degree of inflammation, tension of the fibres, and of pain, than in old ones ; arising, I conceive, from the want of elasticity in the solids, and a tendency to a general relaxed state, either from the hard labour they have before performed, or the debility attending the approach of old age, or from both. I have also observed, that a gross-habited animal, whose action is listless and heavy, who inclines to sleep standing, instead of recumbent in his stall, who is large headed, with a sunken eye, and who is greedy

greedy after water, of which (if he is not checked, he will drink inordinately) is more subject to the grease than the one of a contrary definition. It is more prevalent in winter and spring, than in summer or autumn; in great and close-built towns, than in the country. It is certainly enzootic in Paris, London, Bristol, Amsterdam, and such cities; where most of the causes abovementioned abound: its ravages there are constant and un-remitting; spreading itself more in wet, than in dry and severe frosty weather.

Having proceeded thus far, I shall now enter upon the

C U R E:

Of which great hopes may be entertained when the animal is young; of an active, good habit, and the malady external.

If the subject is plethoric (too full of blood, &c.) the disease not of long standing, yet attended with acrimony, pain, and lameness; begin by bleeding; lessen the quantity of his diet, or rather put him upon a judicious regimen of the mash kind; give him luke-warm blanched water, and nitre, made palatable with honey, or a solution of gum arabic; inject a warm clyster of the decoction of bran, or of mallow-roots; cut off the hair, and then cleanse the parts affected with that argillaceous clay called by the English fullers' earth, finely powdered, and beat into a soft paste with a small quantity of Venice turpentine, hogs' lard, and and the lees of red wine or the grounds of strong beer; put this paste pretty thick, in the form of a cataplasm, upon the sores, so that the whole of the diseased part is well covered with it; let it be secured first by a thick coat of tow, and then by proper rollers, and remain upon the limb at least twenty-four hours; when this dressing is taken off, wash the sores with great care and tenderness, quite clean, with warm milk and water; then apply the turnip poultice, into which put a proper quantity of the extracted juice of saffron and the juice

of

of pounded house-leek: thus continue till you find the running becomes less virulent, and of a more laudable quality; this may generally be effected in a short time; in which case you may indulge the patient with some solid food, and may begin to use the vegetable mineral liquor made warm, but without spirit, to the sores: moderate exercise may also be used, and a smart purge or diuretic given; I prefer the purge first, and that followed by a diuretic. In a day or two, if the sores put on a healthy appearance, and the offensive smell, and ichorous discharge, considerably abate; the vegetable mineral water may be made somewhat stronger; * and assisted by hungary, or double distilled lavender water, or even brandy; but I prefer the use of brandy whey.† Still continue the beforementioned turnip poultice; repeat the purge or diuretic at least once in ten days for three weeks; and lastly, foment the legs all over

by

---

* By an addition of the extract of saturn.

† Thus made, take of milk one part, of water one part: let them boil, then add of brandy till it is turned quite clear.

by flannels dipped in decoction of camomile, alder leaves, or alder bark, rosemary, red rose leaves, and colts-foot leaves. Rowelling in the belly; as also setons at the chest, or upon the inside of the thigh, have been sometimes used about a week from the beginning of this - mode of treatment, and with no small success. Let a necklace* be applied to the horse's neck as early as possible, to prevent him from biting his legs or tearing off the dressings. At this period, if the symptoms are very favourable, you may restore the animal to his usual labour; taking away the poultice; but carefully guarding the sores with tow, wetted in the goulard water, and secured upon the part by a cloth or soft leather; and lastly, by tow dipped in the aloetic tincture of myrrh, instead of goulard water, and secured upon the leg as beforementioned. If a stiffness of the joints, or lameness, arising from obstructions, &c. should remain, let them be well rubbed with warm flannels several times a day; but so as not to

---

* Sold at all sadlers' shops: it is called a horse necklace.

to excoriate the skin. If the subject is old, and this method does not remove it, let the part be fired, and the animal turned out after a proper time. And here let me caution every one against the use of those astringents and repellents, composed of mineral, vitriolic, nitrous, or aluminous ingredients, so much in vogue with common horse doctors; they are sure to produce the evils here before specified; by their drying qualities they repel the humour and throw it back into the habit; thereby vitiating not only the solids, but the fluids: and though the incautious may be amused by empirics with the assurance of a cure; yet but too many have soon found, to their mortification, the disease return, either with a double degree of violence, or make its appearance in a more formidable shape.

I have at times found that purges too much fatigue. I then substitued diuretics or sudorifics: sometimes the milder mode of aperitives; such as the bolus of the powder of the woods; boluses

of

of the powder of gentian, elecampane, and flour of sulphur; preparations of steel or of antimony, or the resins made up with liquorice powder, wheat flour, treacle or honey, into balls; and at times, but with great circumspection, mercurials. If, however, a small drain or running remains after all, do not dry it up by violent applications: it will assist Nature till she recovers her texture and her regular functions; in which she must be aided by great cleanliness and good care in the groom. In order to cure rat-tails, mallenders, and sallenders, frequent dressings, made of burgundy pitch, common frankincense, tar, diachylon, and quicksilver rubbed well down with Venice turpentine, must be applied. Thus also dress the deep chaps or furrows in the pasterns and round the coronet; first clearing them well from dirt, &c. with soft linen, or tow; but if the lips of the chaps appear livid, lay into them some pledgets of tow well soaked in the aloectic tincture of myrrh for a day or two, and then apply the above burgundy pitch cataplasm. In case of trouble-

troublesome warts round the foot, cut them off with a bistoury, and apply a styptic, such as the vitriolic acid, &c. When the bleeding is perfectly staunched, touch the roots of the excrescence with the actual cautery, or the lunar caustic, with the butter of antimony, or the solution of arsenic, &c. When the escar sluffs off, let the wound, if large and very sore, be dressed with the Burgundy pitch cataplasm ; but if small, and disposed to heal, then with a plaister of drying diachylon and cerate only ; repeat these caustics and dressings as often as occasion requires: the nitrous acid in which corrosive sublimate has been dissolved, and the concentrated mineral acid, prove, either of them, very powerful applications in these cases ; but great attention must be given to prevent the inflammation at times raised by the use of them.

If the greasy running humour has, from its virulence, softened the horny texture of the hoof or of the heels or frog, so as to cause the appearance of approaching excrescences

G   called

called fics, &c. let the animal be unshod, cut down the quarters, and the heels of the foot, quite flat, and put on the shorter spectacle shoe,* so that the frog may bear upon the ground as he walks. In this stage of the case, so far as relates to this particular part of the malady, I have known the ægyptiacum alone frequently perform a cure; but it is more certain, if the Burgundy pitch cataplasm is used at intervals.

Great care must be taken not to continue the use of the relaxing system too long, lest it weaken the texture and functions of the skin, promote the growth of warts, augment the putrid diathesis, and bring on a nervous hectic, &c.

If, while pursuing the foregoing methods, an unexpected suppression or stoppage of the humour should take place, whereby lameness, obstruction, and pain, ensues in the limb, together with a loss of appetite, dislike of food, dulness, trembling, &c.

then

No. 7, plate 2, page 199, Lectures.

then it may be feared the humour has reverted from the external to the internal parts of the body; and every effort must be used to bring back the refluent humour to the skin, by immersing the animal in a bath, either of simple water, or medically prepared with herbs or salt, and properly heated;* frictions with brushes, hair-cloth, and flannel, all over the body, both when in and out of it; aromatic and supporting drinks† administered warm on his leaving the bath; and the constant use of the Burgundy pitch cataplasm to the limb: but if, instead of obtaining a running from it, a tumour or abcess should form in the flesh, encourage it by a plaister of the warm gums, and every other skilful means; these tumours being almost always critical, they will

G 2   soon

---

* In addition to this observation on bathing I beg leave to suggest, that much benefit would arise to animals in various diseases if they could be assisted by the operation of a sweating-room.

† By these I mean that excellent preparation and compounded tincture of the Jesuits' Bark, prepared by an eminent English physician, Dr. Huxham, given in red wine either plain or mulled with spices; cordial-drinks, either of simple wine, or of the iufusion of such herbs and roots as do not by their eroding quality, inflame the stomach and intestines.

soon suppurate, and bring about a radical cure. Beware of precipitancy, and cautiously avoid every obstruction to the indications of nature: give her time, and your attention will commonly be crowned with success.

Before I conclude I beg permission to observe, that if the grease is not the forerunner, but proceeding from worms, cachexy, farcy, &c. these disorders must be previously and specifically attended to, and their cure attempted; for, as in these cases the grease is only symptomatic, *it* generally yields to the same medicament, and gradually disappears as the cure of the original malady gains ground.

Having asserted at the beginning of this treatise, that the grease is at times infectious, and at other times contagious; permit me in this place to elucidate this position, by two remarkable instances in the memory of every one. I have premised, that ill-constructed, narrow, wet, or damp

stables,

stables, very much contribute to render this disease infectious. To prove which I lay before you the case of some cavalry which came to Lyons the year before last.* In their route they were under the necessity of stopping at Chalons † and Macon. In the latter town, a muleteer, whose mules had been long and severely afflicted with this disease, was obliged, through necessity, to admit into his stables too large a number of the dragoon horses. The building was little better than a hovel; narrow, confined, and very damp from its being in a bottom. The serjeant farrier, not suspecting the fatal consequences which ensued, suffered these horses to remain thus crouded together in this stable during their stay in the town, separated from the mules by a hand-rail only. On their quitting Macon some slight symptoms of the grease appeared. The usual treatment ment followed; but such was the virulence of it, that not one horse which had stood in the muleteer's

---

* About the year 1770.
† Sur Saone.

teer's stable, nor the horses which afterwards were stalled with them at Lyons, escaped it: and to so alarming a height did it extend, that we were obliged to draft every diseased animal from the troop, and send him to the Montpellier hospital, before its ravages could be stopped.

Thus much for infection. I shall now state as remarkable an instance of contagion. By the long and heavy rains which fell the latter end of last sum_ mer in the district of Lyons,* after a long continuance of dry and sultry weather, the pastures were abundantly saturated with wet ; so that in many places large sheets of stagnate water were formed. These rains, being followed by a return of hot weather, accompanied by a soft southerly wind, the exhalation soon became so noxious as to overload the air of these low grounds. The harvest and vintage had been secured before the setting in of the rain ; the people, rejoicing at the change, had incautiously turned their cattle

* Commonly called the Lyonois.

cattle to graze without taking them under cover at night. The object of the veterinary art being my province alone, I shall confine myself to the disease I am treating of, without saying any thing of the putrid malady, which, from the cause abovementioned, (at that time) so destructively raged amongst the human species. I therefore proceed to remind you, that the principal and governing disease that afflicted the horses, mules &c. was the grease, rapid in its progress, and fatal in its effect. The whole atmosphere seemed tinged with a putrid vapour : men fell by hundreds, and animals by thousands ; the ruminating kind were not exempt from it ; the contagion spread even to and over the mountainous parts of the province : nor did this column of mischief abate its virulent violence till dispersed and destroyed by the purer atmosphere of the Mediterranean Sea, and by a shift of wind, a purer and more elastic air succeeded on land.*

To

* See page 19 Medical Observations.

To conclude, a most exact and unremitting attention is necessary to great cleanliness. Vinegar at proper intervals should be sprinkled, not only in the stable of animals labouring under this and similar diseases, but the mangers and racks should also be frequently washed clean, from the mucus and slaver that adheres to them, with hot water acidulated by vinegar: fresh and pure air should have a well-regulated constant inlet and course throughout the building; very much of the health and recovery of all animals depending upon the succession of oxygen, or pure atmospherical fluid in their stables: exercise, and good dressings with the curry-comb, brushes, hair-cloth, and flannels should never be neglected; nor will it be amiss, if every now and then the inside of the thighs as high as the sheath, and the inside of the fore legs as high as the chest and on each side of it, was to be bathed with water also acidulated with vinegar.

EXPERIMENTS AND OBSERVATIONS

MADE UPON

GLANDERED HORSES,

With intent to elucidate the Rise and Progress of this Disease, in order to discover the proper Treatment of it.

THE Glanders, or that obstruction and corrosion of the lymphatic ducts and fluids in animals who do not cleave the hoof, is a disease at present deemed incurable. Mons. La Fosse is an author much quoted, because highly and deservedly celebrated for his minute and laborious researches into the cause of this disease. He has been at the trouble of dividing

H

it

it into six classes; and of endeavouring to support his reasoning upon them all, sometimes by experiment, and sometimes by analogy: yet I fear he has left us but little to rely on; we are still miserably ignorant as to the cause and nature of this specific virulence, which seems to have baffled all endeavours up to the present moment; it frequently deceives us by putting on appearances and holding out symptoms novel and seducing. The practitioner, thus allured, is buoyed up with hopes of a discovery; he investigates, he applies, he thinks he obtains such lights as lead to elucidation and certainty; but it is all illusion; Hope stands aghast at the disappointment; nor can he fix the proteus till it yields to its more formidable rival Death.

I shall, notwithstanding these discouragements, endeavour to trace the nature of the virus, which has thus baffled all medical application. I shall, at the same time, shew its material difference to the strangles and other diseases of the glands.

Does

Does the virus in the glanders indiscriminately attack all horses exposed to its contact? It does, some few excepted; but in different degrees of virulence, according to their age, food, condition, labour, or local situation: Young horses are more subject to its attack, from the delicacy of their organs; those also who in the stable are fed upon too succulent plants, or herbs full of mucilage, are more liable to it, than they who eat dry food, or graze. Fat horses catch the disease much sooner than lean ones; and the horse at rest more easily than one who is daily at work. Horses who are at large in pastures and fields are seldom attacked; but those which are confined in low and damp stables without a free air, often fall victims to this disease.

Is the infection received by the pores of the skin, or by the breath, the food, or the drink? Experience has proved, that it may be received by one animal rubbing against another, by the breath, and by a sound horse eating the slavered

food

food of a diseased one; but not by water, unless the virus is swallowed with it; neither by inoculating the body with the morbific matter. Diseased stables, foul racks and mangers, and litter upon which a tainted horse has lain, will to a certainty infect a sound animal, if unfortunately he is put into such a situation at the time the disease is active upon the thing infected.

Does the virus in the glanders communicate itself more readily in one season than another? The infection is sooner caught, and the ravages of it more rapid, during the heat of summer, than in the winter; and it is more contagious in the southern countries than in the northern ones.

Does this virus, when working its effects within, and before it appears by a running from the nostrils, produce any visible change in the animal œconomy? No difference has as yet been observed in the animal: the pulse does not vary;

vary; the secretions are regular; the animal does not appear to be depressed; he does not cough; his breathing is free; he, for the most part, preserves his appetite, liveliness, and good condition. When the pituitary membrane begins to be inflamed, and the running appears, no other symptoms of the disease are yet observable; it is only when the virus begins to affect the membranes, the bones, the lymph or crasis of the blood, that the animal's decline is visible.

Is the duration of the disease of any fixed or determined length? No: the horse that labours under it may live from three months to one, two, or three years, and even longer. It is at the same time obvious, that the animal who receives the infection in its last stage of malignancy, will live less time than the one who has caught the disease from a subject in which the virus was less active, and whose constitution was stronger. There are horses, but very few, who can resist the infection altogether.

Are

Are there different sorts of the glanders, as a celebrated author * has asserted? I believe that there only exists one sort, which operates according to its local situation, and the habit of the subject on which it acts; our knowledge in point of natural history extends no farther. The classes, genera, divisions, and sub-divisions of diseases, have occasioned the admission of many errors into medicine relative to human bodies: we should therefore endeavour to preserve that part of the art which respects horses, free from all such errors; which can only be done by admitting as true, that which has been confirmed by experiment; throwing aside whatever is not thus supported by proof, and avoiding all hypothetical systems.

Lastly, is the real seat of disease known? Some place it in the pituitary membrane; some, in the lungs; some, in the lymph; and some, in the external parts of the body. I shall not undertake

* M. La Fosse.

take to reconcile these different opinions ; I will only observe, that if the glanders is caught by the breath or food, I do not conceive why it should stop in its progress at the pituitary membrane, without going down the windpipe and the bronchias; nor do I see any reason why it should not fix upon the lungs. If the existence of the absorbent vessels cannot be denied, can we prove, that the virus deposited on the surface of the pituitary membrane, of the windpipe, or on the bronchias, does not penetrate into the circulation? And if it penetrates thither (as it must, agreeable to the principles of sound philosophy) are we to suppose that it passes through the whole vascular system, without vitiating more or less, the blood and humours in its course, only to obtain a lodgment at the orifices of the excretory vessels of the abovementioned membrane, and corrupt the mucilaginous liquor that flows from thence? It is much more reasonable to conclude, that the virus, circulating through the mass of humours, is particularly affecting and injurious to the lymph ;

that

that Nature provides it a passage through the pituitary membrane ; that the morbific humour flowing upon it, irritates, inflames, and corrodes, producing ulcers : consequently, we should consider this membrane as a proper emunctory destined to throw off the morbific matter, and not as the seat of. the disease. If this opinion is well founded, topical or local remedies are insufficient ; they go to attack only the effect, and not the cause. They become still more inadequate, if the *lymph* or the lungs are affected ; which I have often found to be the case.

Before I proceed to give an account of the symptoms which indicate the glanders, it will be necessary to give a short account of the anatomy of the parts which appear to be more immediately affected by it ; because, without a knowledge of the situation and structure of those parts, it is impossible to distinguish between diseases that are accompanied with many outward symptoms exactly

actly similar ; the practitioner who has not this knowledge, must be constantly liable to form an erroneous opinion of the disease of the animal, which thereby often falls a victim to his ignorance.

A short Description of the Nose and Pituitary Membrane.

THE great cavity of the nose is formed by the union of the maxillary or cheek bones, and the bones of the nose, properly so called. This cavity is divided by a cartilaginous partition (which ossifies in its upper part in old horses) separating the internal parts into two equal cavities, in which are observed three sinuses, namely, the frontal, the maxillary, and the zygomatic sinuses, and four protuberances, like horns, two on each side, called upper and under horns. In these different cavities the infected mucus and other matter is collected, in the glanders, the strangles, and such diseases. It is indispensably necessary, there-

therefore, to have a perfect knowledge of the structure and situation of these different sinuses, in order to ascertain, at first sight, on what part of the surface the operation of trepanning, if necessary, ought to be performed without risk of breaking the partitions that divide them.

The inward cavities of the nose, the sinuses and horns, are lined in their whole extent by the pituitary membrane. This membrane is of considerable thickness upon the cartilaginous partition, but is thinner over the horns and within the sinuses. Its texture is composed of nerves, arteries, veins, and excretory vessels, which proceed from a multitude of glands spread through its whole substance. These nerves are branches of the olfactory nerves, and constitute the organs of smelling. The arterial vessels proceed from a branch of the inward upper carotid artery; and the veinous vessels unite together in order to flow into the jugular vein. In its natural state this membrane is constantly moistened and lubricated

lubricated by a mucilaginous liquor, which defends it against too strong an impression of the air, and preserves it from exication, and a consequent inflammation.

The want of fluidity in the blood and lymph occasions the obstruction of the vessels and glands of the pituitary membrane.

The irritation of the nerves, by producing a contraction of the vessels, contributes to this obstruction.

The relaxation of the texture of the membrane, by depriving the vessels of their tone, occasions a stoppage of the fluid, and produces obstruction.

The inflammation that follows the obstruction is always in proportion to the producing cause. If the cause be local, the inflammation, in many cases, may end by a resolution of the obstructed humours. If it be the effect of a remoter cause,

it

it is more difficult to stop it, and to prevent suppuration of the membrane, especially where the
ulcers are become of a cancerous nature.

Of the Humour running through the Nostrils.

The simple inflammation of the pituitary membrane produces a discharge of a limpid matter,
sometimes slimy, always transparent in the beginning. If the inflammation increases, the stagnated humours become corrupt, and turn to a
thick white pus.

If it lodges and remains in the sinuses, it becomes sharp and corrosive, attacks the bony substance, lacerates the blood-vessels, and this mixed
virus produces a discharge of a yellowish, green,
or bloody appearance.

The flow of matter from the nostrils proceeds
from various causes; which it is very material to
distin-

distinguish, in order not to confound the glanders with other diseases.

A horse in the strangles commonly discharges from the nose a slimy, whitish matter, tinged with yellow (according to the degree of the disorder) resembling that which appears in the glanders. If the strangles are of a bad kind, and the inflammation is carried to its last stage, the matter becomes purulent, sometimes corroding the pituitary membrane, and producing ulcers similar in appearance to those observed in the glanders.

If the strangles are not thoroughly cured, a metastasis frequently takes place, the humour fixes itself on the lungs and forms an abcess.

A horse afflicted with a violent cold* commonly discharges from the nose a humour more or less fluid in the beginning, but which acquires

a

* Morfondure.

a consistency like that of the glanders, so that it is often mistaken for it.

The horse seized with a chest-foundering * commonly discharges at the nose a humour exactly similar to that of the glanders, being viscous, purulent, and sometimes bloody, according to the progress and stages of the disease.

The horse in a confirmed consumption † commonly discharges at the nose a purulent humour, such as that in the glanders. If the matter that comes from the lungs is very sharp, it produces on the pituitary membrane foul and corroded ulcers, of the same nature with those observed in the glanders.

The consumption, being always a consequence of some other disease, is generally attended with a great inflammation in the pleura and the lungs, terminating

* Courbature.
† Pulmonie.

terminating in a suppuration of those parts, which is ejected at the nostrils.

The virus of the grease and farcy also occasions consumptions, by fixing itself upon the lungs, &c. When the running at the nose arises from either of these causes, it is always fatal. I have even seen it, in the hospitals of the veterinary school at Lyons, become contagious.

Analogy of the Symptoms of the Glanders to the above-mentioned Diseases.

WHEN a horse is taken with the glanders, the first external symptom that has yet been discovered is a discharge at the nose, of a limpid, slimy humour. As the disease encreases, this humour changes its consistency and colour; it appears more thick, and tinged with yellow, green, or bloody ichor, &c. such as attends the above diseases: consequently the *colour* of the matter

cannot

cannot be looked upon as a certain characteristic of the glanders, since it is common to these I have just mentioned. I shall therefore endeavour to point out the signs that distinguish those disorders, as well as the symptoms which are *peculiar* to the glanders : And first of the strangles.---

All horses are by nature exposed to the strangles. They are commonly affected with it from two to five years old. A quickened pulse, heaviness, dislike to food, and a cough, are the first symptoms. Soon after, a swelling appears upon the glands of the under jaw, more or less in extent, and more or less inflamed. The parotid, maxillary, and salival glands, are equally swelled. The lymphatic glands are but seldom so.

The morfondure, the sleepy staggers, and lethargy, are the consequences of a checked perspiration, and particularly in the head. In this case the humours flow back to the inward parts, and direct their course towards the pituitary membrane.
The

The symptoms that indicate it are, heat and dryness of the skin ; the pulse, felt at the temporal artery and at the outward maxillary, is tight and deep ; the animal coughs, is dull, and disinclined to food.

The courbature, or chest-foundering, shews itself in the horse by violent fever, the head hanging down, an absolute distaste of food, a difficulty in breathing, a frequent cough, &c.

The Pulmonie, or consumption, begins with a hectic and cough which increases insensibly ; the horse has some appetite till the disease has come to a certain period, when he wastes rapidly, and death soon follows.

Some Symptoms peculiar to the Glanders.

It is remarkable that the virus in most cases of the glanders, does not produce in the begin-

K   ning

ning any sensible alteration in the animal œconomy : the horse taken with it, has neither fever, dulness, or distaste to food ; the appetite is good, the digestion easy, and the secretions regular ; it is precisely this apparent state of health which in part confirms the existence of the glanders when it is attended by the discharge from the nostrils only. The obstruction of the lymphatic glands is a certain token of the virus of the glanders ; but in order to ascertain that fact, it is necessary to know the anatomical structure of those organs, their situation, functions, and connection with the pituitary membrane.

The lymphatic glands of which I am speaking are situated under the tongue, one on each side, within the branches of the under jaw. They receive all the lymphatic vessels that issue from the pituitary membrane, and give rise to a channel, issuing out of them, which reaches the wind-pipe; behind this it descends to the chest, and from thence

thence it empties itself in the left subclavian vein, near the insertion of the thorachic duct. From this short description it may easily be seen, that the glands alluded to must of necessity be obstructed, when the pituitary membrane is ulcerated by the malignancy of the virus; because then the lymph acquires a viscous and thick quality, which renders the circulation more slow, and occasions its obstruction in the glandulous body. Perhaps also the virus contains some noxious and active effluvia, which completes the condensation of the humours. The hardness and insensibility of the glands in this disease in some measure sanctions this idea.

When the discharge is only through one nostril, the gland of that side is alone obstructed; that on the opposite side is not, because the lymphatic vessels which correspond have not yet been attacked by the matter, and the lymph has not yet been completely infected by the virus. The obstruction of the lymphatic glands, one on

K 2

or

or on both sides, is not therefore an unequivocal symptom of the glanders. These glands may be obstructed in other diseases, such as the malignant strangles, &c. beforementioned, wherein the matter acquires a bad quality and corrodes the membrane ; that which comes from the lungs in consumptions, being sharp and corrosive, produces the same effect ; but in these cases we may guard against error, by compressing these glands between our fingers : if, upon so doing, an elastic repulsion is felt from the centre of the glandulous body, and the animal shews sensibility of pain, then it is not the glanders ; in this disease they are hard and quite insensible, as I have already hinted. Without long experience, and a knowledge of the anatomy of these parts, it is impossible for any one to perceive this difference ; although the life of the animal very often depends upon it.

I shall here close my observations, confining them to this short sketch ; my intention being, rather

rather to give an account of some experiments I have made, than to offer an elaborate dissertation on the tubject.

Some Experiments made by me at the Veterinary School at Lyons, whilst I was Professor there.

THE inhabitants of Lyons are obliged by law, to give information to the school, of all horses affected with the glanders, in that city and the adjoining country ; I had consequently daily opportunities of making new experiments ; being at liberty either to kill or preserve the glandered horses, for the instruction of the pupils. It would be unnecessary for me to relate minutely all the trials I made ; but I shall give an account of some, which from their effects I more attentively observed, the journals of which I have kept by me.

EXPERI-

EXPERIMENT I.

THREE horses with the confirmed, ulcerated glanders, discharging copiously at the nostrils, one seven years old, another eight, and a third eleven, were all put in the same stable, and under the following course of medicines.

1st. They were bled at the jugular vein.

2dly. An injection was thrown up their nostils, of lime-water, in which a sufficient quantity of wine vinegar and salt had been mixed.

3dly. Their common food was reduced one third, and they had white water to drink.

4thly. To each was administered six drams of kermes mineral, and three drams of camphire, made into a bolus with flour and honey. The same injection as above was repeated twice a day.
The

The bolus was continued on the 4th, 5th, 6th, and 7th days.

On the 8th day I caused them to swallow in two doses (one in the morning fasting, and the other at night) a quart of red wine, saturated with regulus of antimony. One of the horses began to purge on the 9th day, at 5 o'clock in the morning, and it was over by 3 o'clock in the afternoon ; the second had frequent provocations without voiding at all ; the third did not seem to be any way moved by the medicine. On the same day they were injected with spirit of wine, and water in which copperas and gall-nuts had been infused. On the 10th the injection was repeated again. On the same day they took the bolus with kermes, camphire, and honey.

On the 11th, no medicine whatever was given.

On the 12th, the running at the nose was somewhat abated in all three ; but the pituitary membrane

brane appeared to be more inflamed; the bolus was given.

On the 13th, their food was reduced to half the quantity, the white water was given them in abundance, and an emollient clyster administered to each of them.

On the 14th, the quart of red wine saturated with regulus of antimony.

On the 15th, one of the horses evacuated tolerably well, and the other two very little.

On the 16th, I repeated the injection as above.

17th, The same injection again.

18, 19, 20th, The injection again, and the bolus of kermes, camphire, and honey. The discharge was much diminished in the first and second horses; but still abundant in the third, through

one

one of the nostrils only. The lymphatic glands were still in the same condition.

21st, 22d, 23d, 24th, The Bolus and injections were continued.

On inspection of the urine and dung, there was a strong indication of great heat in the blood; consequently I suspended the course of medicines, till the 30th day. In the interval they had plenty of white water to drink.

On the 31st the urine and stools appeared to be in a healthy, natural state.

32d, The bolus was continued. Injections were made with allum and white vitriol, mixed together over the fire, afterwards reduced to powder, and dissolved in lime-water; to which was added a sufficient quantity of vinegar.

33d, 34th, The injection was repeated twice a day, and the bolus continued.

L

35th, The running disappeared in one of the horses.

40th, The running ceased in the second. The bolus and injections were continued every other day only. The general treatment was continued with the third, to the 55th day. The running ceased in him also after two months, from the first beginning. A stop was now put to all medicines. The obstruction of the glands was removed also in one of the horses, and remained very little discernible in the other two. At this time, thinking it to be a secondary effect of the disease, and supposing that the resolution was only in the conglobated glands, I imagined that time would complete the cure. Every thing seemed to promise it until the 72d day, when the running appeared anew in one ; it shewed itself at the end of three weeks in the second ; and near three months elapsed before it returned in the third horse ; in all of them it was more violent than ever. The two former

former were first killed for investigation. I found the frontal and maxillary sinuses filled with purulent matter in both ; the pituitary membrane was also ulcerated in many places ; from whence I inferred, that the injections had not penetrated into the superior cavities. On inspection, the back part of the mouth, the windpipe, the bronchias, and the lungs, discovered no mark of inflammation : all the other parts appeared in their natural state. Tthe third was afterwards killed and opened : I found that the frontal, maxillary, and zygomatic sinuses, contained much bloody matter ; the membrane was ulcerated to a great degree ; the bones carious in many parts ; and the lymphatic gland on the right side was become schirrous ; I found in the right lobe of the lungs five vomicas the bigness of a pigeon's egg, or nearly so. No other part seemed to be affected.

L 2

EXPERI-

EXPERIMENT II.

Two saddle-horses (the one Spanish, the other Navarese; the former nine years old, the latter seven) in the confirmed glanders, were put under the following regimen.

They were restricted to a low diet for two days, and let blood the third. The 4th day they were trepanned; the Spanish horse on the left side, because the running was only there. The operation was performed on both sides the head of the Navarese; the matter being discharged from both his nostrils. After the operation, I injected through the openings a decoction of barley water and honey, to cleanse the ulcers.

The 5th, I used the injection made with lime-water, vinegar, and salt. It was repeated twice.

The

The 6th, I gave to each four quarts of the second lime-water, sweetened with honey. This drink, and the injections, were continued to the 15th day.

The 16th, the running had diminished one half; but the obstruction of the lymphatic glands was augmented.

The 17th, the running became more abundant; but the matter seemed to be of a better sort. The lime-water was continued to the 30th, in the proportion of six quarts a day. The horses now becoming dull, and disgusted with their food, I suspended the course of medicines till the 35th day.

The 36th, two quarts a day of a strong infusion of camomile was given to each. This was continued to the 42d. The dulness disappeared; their appetite returned; but the discharge, as well as the obstruction of the glands, continued the same.

The 43d, in the morning, I threw up injections with honeyed barley water; in the afternoon, a second injection with allum, white vitriol, lime-water, and vinegar, was administered. This was continued to the 50th day. At that time the matter was whitish, and in small quantity; but the Spanish horse now discharged pus at both nostrils.

From the 51st to the 60th, injections were given, made with spirit of wine, copperas, and gall-nuts.

The 66th, the running had almost disappeared; both horses were in good spirits, and eat and drank as usual. They were walked out an hour every day.

The Spanish horse soon seemed to be well, and continued so about amonth; after which time the running appeared again; the matter became bloody and foetid. Convinced now of the inefficacy of remedies

medies to him, he was killed. On opening the nose, I observed the membrane was corroded, particularly on the right side; the superior horn was almost destroyed, and the lachrymal duct choaked up with purulent matter. The dissection of the brain offered nothing particular. The viscera of the abdomen was sound. A small portion of the interlobulary texture of the lungs had abcesses; but the matter had not penetrated into the bronchias. The lymphatic glands contained a concreted humour.

The Navarese preserved (to all appearance) perfect health from the beginning of June to the end of August in the same year. At that period the running took place again; and in thespace of three weeks the disease increased to such a degree, that I was obliged to kill the animal. On opening, I observed that the pituitary membrane was ulcerated in a great extent of its surface; the cartilaginous partition was attacked by the matter; the sinuses contained very little of it. All the intestines appeared sound.

EXPERIMENT III.

A large cart-horse, ten years old, having the lymphatic gland on the right side much obstructed, hard, and insensible, the membrane ulcerated, with a discharge of yellowish and fœtid matter, was put upon the following course.

1st, The animal was reduced to bran and white water for food ; and was bled *twice in the* space of two days. On the 3d I performed the operation of the trepan in two places ; and injected into the nazal foveas and sinuses, a strong decoction of wormwood. The injection was continued for six days with the addition of honey.

The 10th, the injection was made with the second lime-water. It was continued to the 15th.

The 16th, 3 drams of Ethiops mineral, incorporated with honey, were given. The injections

jections were made with the first lime-water, and continued to the 24th, as also the bolus, with an addition of a dram of Æthiops mineral. At that period the running was diminished one half, and the matter had become more laudable. I continued the same course of medicine to the 40th.

The 41st, the running was almost suppressed, and the size of the gland considerably diminished; the injections and the bolus were continued to the 50th, when the running ceased. The injection was now repeated only every other day; the bolus was reduced to two drams.

The 61st, I discontinued all medicine, and soon after the horse was gradually brought to his usual quantity of food. He was placed in another stable; his dress was changed; he was looked after by another groom, and walked out everyday in an enclosed place; during which time his former stable was well washed, and fumigated with brimstone, gunpowder, spirit of vitriol, and juniper berries.

M   All

All these precautions, however, did not prevent the running at the nose from returning at the end of three weeks : the animal was then killed. On open ing him, the nostrils exhibited the membrane ulce- rated in three or four places only. One of them, which was broad and deep, had attacked the bony substance. The sinuses contained much yellowish matter, mixed with bloody filaments, produced by the dilaceration of the small vessels. Part of the villous membrane of the stomach was slightly in- flamed ; the cardiac orifice was a little more so ; the inflammation had also reached the slender intestines ; the left lobe of the lungs was in- flamed, and filled with a black, thick blood : this might be either the consequence of the Æthiops mineral, or of the virus of the glanders.

EXPERIMENT IV.

Two Danish coach-horses, the one seven years old, the other eight : the first was in the con- firmed

firmed glanders; the second with the same disorder, but at that stage which we at present deem its beginning only. They were placed in two separate stables, and put under the following course.

1st, They were kept without hay for some days, and had bran and white water for food.

2dly, They were blooded at the jugular vein; and to each two emollient clysters were given.

3dly, A decoction of mallows, marsh-mallows, pellitory, elder-flowers, and camomile, was injected into the nostrils.

4thly, The horse which was most infected was made to swallow a bolus, composed of four drams of mercury, and as much cream of tartar, incorporated in a sufficient quantity of honey. The other horse took a bolus composed of two drams of precipitate *per se*, or the precipitate of

M 2

mercury,

mercury, incorporated with honey. The injections, clysters, and boluses, were continued to the 20th.

The 21st, the running was much increased in the former; the matter also began to grow brown and bloody at intervals; and the obstruction in the lymphatic glands was enlarged. In the latter, the running was less abundant; the matter was clear and transparent; the glands less hard and voluminous. The same course was followed and adhered to in both till the 30th.

The 31st, the running had stopped in the latter; the course of medicines. was continued a week afterwards to him.

The 36th, I performed the operation of trepanning upon the former. The cavities were injected with lime-water; afterwards, the injections were used which I have mentioned in the first and second experiment. I suspended the use of the

the bolus, the evacuations being so great, they made me apprehend a disorder in the stomach.

I continued the injections till the 65th day. The running appeared and disappeared at different times, and at last became constant, and of a bad sort. As the animal fell away rapidly, I thought proper to kill it. On opening the body, nothing particular appeared, except an infinite number of little ulcers on the pituitary membrane. The sinuses contained but little matter. The other horse appeared to be radically cured; which I ascribed to the good habit of the animal's body, the small quantity of the virus, its lesser degree of malignancy, and the short time it was allowed to ravage, rather than to the course of medicines. Besides, in these matters, a single fact cannot establish any thing.

EXPERI-

EXPERIMENT V.

A saddle-horse, about eleven years old, newly attacked, as I was informed, with the glanders, was treated in the following manner.

1st, He was let blood, confined to white water, and had several emollient clysters administered for three days.

2dly, He was treated exactly as the horse which I last mentioned to have been cured; but the success was not the same : for, after three months' perseverence, I was obliged to kill him. On opening, I found the pituitary membrane ulcerated, but nothing else.

EXPERIMENT VI.

A saddle-horse of the Limousin, aged nine years, with the confirmed glanders, which had

made

made some progress, was put under the same course of medicines as the preceding one, for ten weeks. At that period the remedies had worked no good effect : the discharge was abundant, bloody, and fœtid ; the breathing became extremely laborious : in short, all the signs of death appeared, and the animal shortly expired. On opening, the nostrils exhibited the same appearances which I had observed in other horses ; but, in proceeding farther in the dissection of the mouth and wind-pipe, I perceived that the running proceeded in a great degree from the lungs, within which I found a collection of fœtid pus, mixed with the humour of the bronchias, arising from ulcerations, with which that viscera was attacked. I now thought that I had mistaken the real characteristic of the disease, and that the animal had died of a consumption ; but, as it was equally possible that the virus in the glanders had produced those effects, I suspended my judgment, waiting by new experiments to elucidate it.

EXPERI-

EXPERIMENT VII.

As the efficacy of Æthiops mineral and peri-winkle in the glanders had been much spoken of, I embraced the first opportunity to make trial of the virtue of each.

Three hackney coach-horses, eight, nine, and eleven years old, affected with the glanders nearly in the same degree, were treated in the following manner.

1st, They were all three prepared for evacuation, with white water and emollient clysters; a purge was then given them, composed of one ounce of aloes, two drams of sweet mercury, two ditto of jalap, two ditto of cream of tartar; the whole mixed with honey. The next day they evacuated pretty well.

The

The 3d day, they took one ounce of Æthiops mineral, and one ounce of powder of periwinkle.

The 4th, they were trepanned on one side; the cavities of the head were injected with vulnerary water; the Æthiops mineral, and periwinkle powder was continued to all the three, to the 10th day; and the injection was the same as on the 4th.

The 11th, the purge was administered as before mentioned.

The 12th, they purged very well. The 13th and 14th, all medicine was suspended, except the injection.

The 15th, they returned to the use of Æthiops and periwinkle. The course of medicine was the same till the end of the 24th day.

The 25th and 26th, no medicines were administered; but white water and clysters were

N   given.

given. At that period the running of matter was diminished in one; but it was increased in the two others.

The 27th, they took the usual medicine.

The 28th, they purged rather too much.

The 29th, they seemed dejected, dull, and disgusted with food. I therefore suspended all operations till the 35th, when I repeated the injections. On the 36th, the appetite came again. On the 37th, the Æthiops, periwinkle, and injection, were continued to the 45th. The 46th and 47th, I left them quiet. The running diminished sensibly in the first; it had even disappeared for three days; but it continued still in the two others. The lymphatic glands were in the same degree of fulness.

The 48th, the medicine was given them; but the jalap was omitted, in order to substitute in its place three drams of nitre.

The

The 49th, one of the three purged very little; the other two not at all. They seemed very dull, nauseated their food, and more changed than usual. I ascribed those symptoms to inflammation in the stomach and intestines, occasioned by the use of the medicines; in consequence of this, I left them quiet till the 58th day. On the 60th, I renewed the use of Æthiops and periwinkle; which was continued to the 70th. At the end of that time, the glanders appeared to me to be incurable in the two last; they therefore were killed. On opening their nostrils, I discovered nothing new: the pituitary membrane was ulcerated, as in most of those I had already opened; the pleura and the lungs seemed to be sensibly inflamed; the inflammation was greater in the villous membrane of the stomach, in the pilorus, and the smaller intestines. The first horse seemed to be in a fair way of recovery: the matter was transparent, and in small quantity; I soon found means to suppress the running altogether, by injections of prime lime-water. The

N 2

usual

usual medicines were continued till the 96th. The next day, the Æthiops and periwinkle were discontinued; but the animal was still purged three times in the space of a month. I then returned him to his master, seemingly in very good health; but he sent him back to me at the end of two months, with every appearance of the glanders. I renewed the former treatment for the space of six weeks to no purpose; the animal was then killed and opened. I discovered many cankers in the pituitary membrane; and found that many had been cicatrized by means of the injections. If, as I had reason to think, all those which now appeared were new ones, it proves that the seat of the glanders is not local, but exists generally in the mass of humours.

EXPERIMENT VIII.

FOUR fine cart-horses, having caught the glanders on the road from Nismes to Lyons, were brought

brought to the veterinary school. I put them upon the same treatment as I have just described, without obtaining better success. They were killed at the expiration of two months. The dissection of their bodies furnished nothing deserving of notice.

EXPERIMENT IX.

A Navarese horse, nine years old, in the confirmed glanders, was put under the treatment above-mentioned, but without being trepanned. The second medicine, administered on the 2d day, gave him a cholic, which was followed by a super-purgation. He immediately swallowed an astringent drink, composed of one ounce of diascordium, one ounce of prepared chalk, and two ounces of honey, boiled in three pints of red wine. This drink was repeated four times in twenty-four hours, but without success. The animal died on the 3d day. I discovered, on opening the nose, that the pituitary membrane

was

was ulcerated on the right side only. The zygomatic sinus was filled with whitish and purulent matter. The lungs were slightly inflamed ; but the intestines and the stomach were much more so. This last observation proves, that the animal was of a very irritable disposition of body ; and that the cathartics had been a real poison to him ; as they generally are to all horses, if not administered with the greatest caution.

EXPERIMENT X.

Two horses, the one an English hunter, the other a Neapolitan manage-horse ; the first ten years old, the second twelve, having contracted the glanders in the same stable, were submitted to the following treatment.

1st, I caused the hair of both to be shaved, from the neck down to the buttocks, and as low on each side as the middle of the body.

2dly,

2dly, I caused emollient fomentations to be applied all over the body for the space of a week.

3dly, I employed frictions of mercurial ointment over the buttocks, about one ounce at a time; which I continued every other day for twelve days.

4thly, I made four frictions on the rump, by one ounce and a half of ditto every other day.

5thly, I made two frictions on the loins, with the same dose as the preceding one, and in the same interval of time.

The 21st day, the symptoms had not varied.

The 22d the parotids began to swell.

The 23d, the maxillary glands were in the same condition. The frictions were made on the back, from the loins to the withers.

The

The 24th, all the parts of the head were greatly swelled in the Neapolitan, and salivation began to take place.

The 25th, he could not open his jaws ; I therefore let him blood twice the same day. I repeatedly injected into his mouth barley water with honey; and I gave him, the same night, a laxative clyster, composed of four ounces of catholicon, dissolved in boiling water. The injections in the mouth were continued every two hours during the night.

The 26th, the same injections, and a purging clyster.

The 27th, 28th, 29th, and 30th, the same treatment was continued ; the salivation was abundant ; but the stricture in his jaws was taken off on the 28th.

The 31st, the obstruction in the glands began to diminish ; and the animal drank water with nitre dissolved in it.

The 32d, the injections, and the nitrated drink, were continued to the 40th.

The 41st, the running at the nostrils had increased; but the fulness of the head, and salivation, were less. The animal was left quiet till the 46th day.

The 47th, I renewed the frictions, in doses of an ounce; they were continued to the 57th.

The 58th, the fulness of the head took place again, and the salivation became copious. I reduced both by the same means I had before employed. The obstruction and salivation were not so considerable in the English horse. After having left them quiet for a month, I perceived that the glanders had increased in malignity. I went on another month, but without success. I then caused the two animals to be killed. The opening of the nose exhibited, in a greater degree, the same ravages I have so often mentioned.

o The

The inside of the mouth was a little inflamed; the excretory ducts of the salivary glands were increased in size.

EXPERIMENT XI.

A charger, nine years old, with a fresh infection, was subjected to the same treatment as the two preceding ones. After the eleventh friction, the fulness of the salivary glands became so considerable, the blood flowed to the head with such impetuosity, that it was impossible for me to prevent the consequences. The animal died within twenty-four hours. It was not opened. Four other horses were subjected, in the course of the same year, to the treatment of mercurial frictions, but without success.

EXPERIMENT XII.

A large draft-horse, seven years old, suspected of having the glanders for six weeks, and which had

had been previously under the care of a common farrier, was brought to the veterinary school, and treated as follows.

1st, He was blooded at the jugular vein, received some emollient clysters, and tasted nothing but white water during the space of twenty-four hours.

2dly, Volatile alkali, or spirit of sal-ammoniac, was given, mixed with an infusion of angelica-róot; taking care to keep him well covered in a warm stable. This first dose quickened the circulation, and increased the degree of heat over the whole body, without exciting perspiration. The next day I encreased the dose of alkali two drams; still using the infusion of angelica. The drink was given at six o'clock in the morning; at eight the pulse was high; at ten the perspiration was perceptible; at twelve the sweat was copious, and continued till six o'clock at night. Two emollient clysters were given in the course

of

of the night.   His drink was just coloured with wheat bran.   This treatment was observed for the three following weeks.   At that period I discontinued the drink for a week ; but the clysters were still given.   The 25th day, the running had a little diminished ; but the lymphatic glands were harder.

The 32d, the running was trifling ; the matter began to be transparent.

The 33d, I renewed the use of volatile alkali in the infusion of angelica ; which produced only a small perspiration.   On the same day, the nostrils were injected with a decoction of centaury, and gentian, to which was added a small quantity of vulnerary-water, and continued till the 44th. During all this time the sweats were sufficiently copious ; the urine in small quantity, and of a reddish tint ; the excrements hard and dry, in spite of the daily use of emollient clysters and white water.   As the animal was much wasted, and

and appeared weak, I left him to himself till the 54th; when the injections were continued, but with lime-water.

The 62d, the running disappeared entirely. The injections were continued for a week; at the end of which the medicines were discontinued. All this time, the cloths which covered the animal were washed and shifted every day; the greatest cleanliness was also observed in every other respect. At the end of a month, he was sent to grass in a low and marshy place; but, after two months, the glanders returned, and he was killed. I had no opportunity of opening him.

EXPERIMENT XIII.

FOUR horses, of various ages, differently diseased with the glanders, were successively treated in the method just described; but without any success. The opening of the bodies presented nothing extraordinary.

EXPERI-

EXPERIMENT XIV.

A large Swiss horse, seven years old, employed in drawing boats on the river Rhone, having the confirmed glanders, was treated as follows.

1st, He was dieted for 24 hours, after which I made him take a dose, composed of six drams of aloes, two drams of jalap, one dram of sweet mercury, five drams of nitre, incorporated in a sufficient quantity of honey. Two days after the purge, I made an incision in the chest; in which I introduced half an ounce of corrosive sublimate, which produced a temporary choaking. The running (of a reddish serosity, which commonly takes place after such an operation) became very abundant in a few days, because the horse was fat, and full of humours.

2dly, I caused him ·to swallow of liver of sulphur half an ounce, incorporated with two ounces
of

of honey; injections of lime-water were administered to him twice every day.

This treatment was adhered to for the space of six weeks; at which time the running had almost ceased. It seemed, that the evacuation of the humour by the chest had occasioned a sort of derivation, or revulsion. In place of the liver of sulphur, a bolus of balsam of turpentined sulphur was now given. It was continued for a month; at the end of which the horse had no running, and seemed to be well. He remained in that condition for two months, when the disease appeared again in a slight degree. The animal lived three years in the infirmary, where he served to carry out the bodies for dissection. He died of a consumption, the common consequence of inveterate glanders.

EXPERIMENT XV.

I followed the treatment above mentioned with five other horses, without having the good fortune

of

of curing one of them ; the particulars therefore do not deserve to be related. I have restored many horses who were thought by some to be glandered, because they had no certain criterion for ascertaining the true glanders ; but I readily confess, that I do not believe I ever succeeded, but in one instance, to a complete cure of that disease, although nobody, perhaps, has ever made more attempts to attain it.

On Innoculation, of the glandered Virus into sound Animals, by contact, &c.

ESSAY I.

Two sound horses, the one fresh from grass, aged six years, and the other nine years, just come from work, were placed by a horse who had the glanders, drinking out of the same pail, and eating at the same manger. The first shewed evident

evident signs of the glanders at the expiration of 34 days. It fully declared itself in the second at the end of six weeks.

ESSAY II.

Two horses in good health, the one seven, the other eleven years old, both just taken from work, were placed by a horse who had the glanders. The former caught the disease, and ran at the nostrils, 52 days afterwards; the second, in three months.

ESSAY III.

A horse thirteen years old, very lean, was made to drink the same water out of the same pail with a horse who had the glanders, and continued so to do for two months; but kept from the diseased animal during that time; he did not catch it.

P   ESSAY

ESSAY IV.

A horse, nine years old, in tolerable condition, placed by a horse who had the glanders in the last stage of the disorder, caught it at the end of 43 days.

ESSAY V.

THREE old horses, destined to the anatomical investigations of the school, having been inoculated with the virus in the neck, did not catch the disease. This experiment was repeated on various horses of all ages, without producing any effect. It was also performed upon an ox, a sheep, and a dog, without impairing in the least the health of those animals.

ESSAY VI.

THE coverings and saddles that had been used to glandered horses, being placed on several horses in good health for a month, and during the heat of summer, did not convey the distemper.

ESSAY VII.

THE virus, mixed with a little flour, given to three horses for the space of a week, communicated the disease to the youngest at the end of a month. The two others did not sicken till some time after.

By multiplying such experiments only, we shall be able,

1st, To ascertain the degree of infection of the glanders.

2dly, To discover the first symptoms by which it is announced; and which have escaped our notice to this day.

P 2

LASTLY,

L A S T L Y,

As we should, by such means, be certain of attacking it in its origin, we might attain to a probable method of cure: for, notwithstanding my failures, I think that a remedy may be found for the glanders. The animal, vegetable, and mineral kingdoms, abound with an infinite number of substances; the combination and rational application of which will, perhaps, in time overcome those obstacles which have hitherto opposed the progress of the veterinary art, in many diseases. Discoveries wait only favourable opportunities to disclose themselves; and the most favourable are those which are furnished by scientific associations, extending their patronage and encouragement for the perfection of the arts.*

I

---

* The Board of Agriculture, first planned by Sir John Sinclair, Bart. and now established under the sanction of Parliament, bids fair to be of the greatest national utility in this, as well as in every other branch of improvement and discovery.

I shall here conclude the account of my experiments; and shall only observe, that those I made when professing comparative anatomy at Montpellier have convinced me, that the virus of the glanders has more activity in the south than in the north; that its progress is more rapid in the mule and the ass, than in the horse; but that they are not so subject to receive it by infection or contact.

SHORT OBSERVATIONS

ON THE

CHOLIC, OR GRIPES;

MORE PARTICULARLY THAT KIND TO WHICH RACE-
HORSES ARE LIABLE.

THE irritation of the nervous fibres, and the contraction of the capillary vessels, distributed throughout the intestines; and the obstructions produced in those vessels by the stagnation of the blood and humours; occasion the pains in the abdomen which are called the cholic, or gripes.

As

As the causes which produce these ailments are very various, it becomes indispensably necessary to distinguish them, in order to administer the remedy best adapted to each case.

The particular causes of cholic are,

First, crude and acrimonious substances in the stomach or intestines, occasioned by the bad quality of food, or by the weakness of the organs of digestion.

Secondly, an indigestion, arising from too great repletion in the stomach.

Thirdly, the excrements growing dry, and continuing too long in the intestines.

Fourthly, wind confined within the intestines.

Fifthly, cold water given to a horse while in a great heat and sweating.

Sixthly,

Sixthly, different kinds of worms in the stomach and intestines.

Seventhly, the effect of some strange body, as hair-balls, bezoar-stones, &c.

Lastly, an injudicious use of purgative medicines.

All these several causes produce a greater or less degree of inflammation in the abdomen; which discovers itself by different symptoms; some are common to all disorders of the kind, and some are peculiar to its specific species.

A horse seized with a common cholic appears in great agitation; he frets, lies down, and rises again; strikes the ground with his fore feet; and is always shifting his position.

There are, besides, some particular symptoms, which serve to characterize the specific disorder,

Q

and

and to guide the practitioner in the choice of the medicines he ought to employ to subdue it.

If a horse is attacked with a cholic proceeding from indigestion, soon after feeding upon too much corn, or any other food, besides the general symptoms already described, the breathing will become difficult and laborious, attended with apparent great heaviness; he will groan, and repeatedly stretch out his head and neck.

A cholic proceeding from wind is easily discovered. The horse will be afflicted with great tension of the belly, which is more or less inflated by the rarification of the air contained in the intestines; he will have frequent ventose discharges, attended with restlessness, great pain, and perpetual shiftings.

Cholics which are occasioned by worms are not equally painful; neither is the horse equally disturbed, as by ordinary cholics; yet his appetite
fails;

fails; he grows thinner daily; and is continually extending his body, by stretching his fore legs forward, as if he was desirous of bringing his belly to the ground.

The *red cholic* * is the most dangerous of all the kinds to which a horse is liable. It is called by that name on account of the inflammation; which in that case is carried to the extreme degree; and makes so rapid a progress, that mortification takes place in the affected parts of the abdomen within the space of a few hours. The most vigilant attention, therefore, must be given, to distinguish this malady from every other sort of cholic, in order to administer the speediest assistance possible.

A horse seized with this species of the cholic is much more agitated than in any other case of the disorder. He not only lies down repeatedly, immediately rises again, and strikes the ground

Q 2   with

* La tranchée rouge.

with his feet ; but is continually turning his head towards his flanks and belly ; he discovers signs of pain, if either of them is pressed hard ; the conjunctive membrane of the eye appears very much inflamed ; the sphincter of the anus is in the same condition, and it appears of a bright red.

This great degree of inflammation, which takes place in the red cholic, is always in some degree occasioned by the acrimony of the bile, but particularly by immoderate use of purgatives given too often, and in too large doses.

It is a known fact, that very many medicines of this class act as internal blisters, irritating the nervous fibres of the stomach and intestines ; and when they operate with too much activity, they irritate also the extremities of the capillary blood-vessels, cause them to contract, and stop the passage of the blood, by which inflammation is produced.   To this must be added the distension of the

the blood-vessels, causing the compression of the nervous system, from whence the great pain under which the animal so much suffers arises.

Such is the effect of violent purgatives; and I will even venture to assert (and to maintain the assertion) *that they are the principal causes of cholics in race-horses.* I shall, on this subject, take the liberty of making a short digression, and observe, That the question is not yet determined, whether purgatives ought or ought not to be at all used in veterinary medicine; that we are entirely ignorant of their relation to the organization of the horse; that experience has hitherto shown, in the different veterinary schools, that there are but very few cases in which these medicines appear to be required; and, that the greatest prudence is at all times necessary in the use of them.

In fact, if we consider the horse either as an herbivorous or granivorous animal, and consider also the simplicity and uniformity of the food by which

which it is sustained, we shall easily apprehend, that it cannot have the same need of artificial evacuations, by means of purgatives, as man, whose intemperence, in every respect, continually opposes and counteracts the direct and uniform process of nature.

What is whimsical enough, it is not the diseased horse only which is purged ; but that also which is in perfect health ; and this, it seems, with the view of making him lighter and more speedy.

If we were to enquire the cause of this conduct upon the course, I fear the answer given would not be grounded on principles of sound and approved science ; and they who were unequal to support the custom by reason, must shelter themselves under the example of their forefathers, from whom they received it to transmit it equally unaccounted for to the use of their posterity.

The

The greater part of those established principles which have obtained in human medicine, have been determined by means of the relation subsisting between patients and their physicians; and by certain effects of remedies taken, and from which such and such sensations had been experienced, of which the patients were able to give an account. But veterinary medicine is entirely destitute of this resource; the patient cannot co-operate with the physician by the means of speech. If he had that faculty, he would probably, when afflicted with the red cholic, express himself thus: You have purged me too violently, and in too large doses; when no necessity existed, you conveyed a fire into my stomach and blood; from whence results the present evil, which marks me the martyr of your ignorance; and while you are drenching me with cordials, under the expectation of giving me relief, you are but encreasing the violence of my tortures. But, to return,

Cholics

Cholics occasioned by drinking cold water, while hot, are the least dangerous ; all that seems requisite is to keep the horse well co-vered, to bleed him, and to administer emollient glysters.

I shall say nothing, in this place, of hepatic cholics ; I shall also decline speaking of those which are produced by hair-balls, or any other concretion ; because they are incurable. I shall confine myself to the indication of some re-medies for cholics to which race-horses are liable; such, namely, as proceed from the effervescence or acrimony of the bile, the use of violent purges, wind, and sometimes worms.

As every sort of cholic is accompanied with inflammation, it is necessary, in the first place, to bleed ; which must be repeated according to the violence of the pain, and the degree of fever and inflammation. The horse should then be made to swallow half a pint, or rather better, of oil

of

of castor; and a loosening and softening drink should be made, composed of mallows, marsh-mallows, mullein or cows-lungs wort *(verbascum,)* bears-breech *(acanthus,)* pellitory, lettuce, all-good, or English mercury *(mercurialis,)* and sorrel, a handful of each ; the whole boiled together, in six quarts of water, twenty minutes, and this decoction given luke-warm, one quart every two hours.   The same decoction is also to be administered in a clyster, to which may be added some cold drawn linseed oil.   It is necessary to cleanse the large intestines; because the fœces which lodge there keep up the inflammation in the abdomen.

This method of treatment is proper to be observed in the beginning of every sort of cholic, except that which proceeds from indigestion because it would, in that case, weaken the powers of digestion, and endànger the animal's life.   Instead, therefore, of the above prescription, we must give a dose of theriaca, dissolved in a pint

of

good red wine ; or 3 ounces of elixir proprietatis, mixed with the same quantity of geneva, to which add a pint of warm strong beer ; after which, the horse should be smartly trotted some time, and in about two hours let him have a gallon of luke-warm water to drink, but no rack or manger meat till an hour after his water.   It is to be observed, that old horses are more liable to cholics proceeding from indigestion than young ones.

In windy cholics, give the elixir proprietatis, &c. as above prescribed, or the following drink. Take seed of cummin and anise-seed, of each one ounce and a half ; the root of masterwort *(im-peratoria,)* and angelica, of each one handful ; let them boil eight or ten minutes in three quarts of plain water ; divide them into two doses ; which give at the interval of one hour ; take also a head of garlic, or an onion, and a piece of soap, about the size of an egg, pound them together in a mortar, and add two pinches of pepper ; make them into the form of a soft bolus, insert it

into

into the rectum as far as you are able, and make the horse walk about for half an hour; after which, administer a clyster, consisting of one ounce of black soap, dissolved in a pint of warm water. If the pain should still continue, and the belly appear more swelled and tender, it will be necessary to draw a little blood.

If the cholic is occasioned by worms, after having employed the general remedies we have described, we must have recourse to the elixir proprietatis, geneva, and strong beer, and the next day to the use of bitters. Accordingly we must prepare a drink, consisting of a decoction of wormwood, fern, lesser centaury, and gentian, and give it in a dose of two quarts a day fasting, to be continued until such time as the animal ejects the worms together with his excrements.

In the red cholic, we should confine ourselves rigidly to relaxing and anodyne remedies; we should therefore give drinks made with emollient plants, as directed page 123, together with linseed,

oil of castor, and emollient clysters. Bleeding
may be repeated frequently if necessary, and the
English antimonial preparation, *pulvis jacobus* administered every six hours. The horse must be
kept warm, and also to a severe regimen; he must
be allowed nothing but nitrated water whitened
and made pretty good with oat or barley meal.

If, notwithstanding this treatment, the pain
should still continue with violence, we may
hazard sixteen or twenty grains of opium; although I confess it is with fear that I propose
this remedy; because it is not always attended
with good effects; and also because it is both very
difficult to seize the moment when it should be
used, and to proportion the quantity to the actual
state of the disorder. If the dose is too weak,
the cholic is rendered the more violent; if, on
the other hand, it is too strong, it will hasten the
animal's death. The veterinary physician alone
is competent to judge, from the state of the pulse
and other symptoms, of the effects which the use
of opium is likely to produce.

If the malady should resist the power of all these remedies, and the following symptoms appear, it generally proves fatal.

The horse remains on his legs as long as he possibly can; he is afraid of lying down; he makes several attempts before he accomplishes it; however, he presently rises again, preferring to stand thus painfully tottering on his feet, rather than subject his whole frame to the agony of a recumbent position. At this period a profuse sweat comes over the whole body; a general tremor takes place; the breathing is quick and interrupted; the nostrils much dilated; the pituitary membrane, and that of the mouth and gums, are of a livid colour; the lips are cold; the yard is sometimes relaxed, and the urine distills drop by drop. In this deplorable state, a mortification takes place, and death is inevitable.

F I N I S.

CONTENTS OF THE POSTHUMOUS WORKS.

E R R A T A.

A very severe and long illness having prevented the Editor from that close attention he would otherwise have shown to the *literal* correctness of the press, in the posthumous parts of this work, &c. he humbly entreats the indulgent Reader will look over such errors as he may discover on perusal.

THE

POSTHUMOUS WORKS

OF

CHARLES VIAL DE SAINBEL,

CONSISTING OF

GENERAL OBSERVATIONS

ON THE

ART OF VETERINARY MEDICINE;

AN ESSAY ON THE GREASE,

OR WATERY SORES IN THE LEGS OF HORSES;

WHICH OBTAINED THE PRIZE GIVEN BY THE ROYAL SOCIETY OF MEDICINE.

AN ESSAY ON THE GLANDERS;

AND

OBSERVATIONS ON THE GRIPES.

LONDON:

PRINTED FOR

J. WRIGHT, 169, PICCADILLY.

1797.

EXPLANATION OF THE PLATES.

No. I.

THE frontispiece, representing a groom holding a horse's foot.

No. II.

The Veterinarian, explaining to the Farrier the natural shape of the foot, and the form of a shoe proper for it.

No. III.

Ignorance running away, with a mask in her hand.

PLATE I.

Fig. A.   *Represents a leg well jointed.*

Fig. B.   ——— *a leg too long jointed.*

Fig. C.   ——— *a leg too short jointed.*

Fig. D. D.   ———*feet turning outwardly, called in French, panard.*

Fig. EE.   ———*feet turned inwardly, called in French, cagneux.*

Fig. F. G.   ———*a leg describing a circle of 25 degrees, and the foot supposed to be shod with the new concave shoe.*

Fig. H. I.   ———*a leg, the foot supposed to be shod with a flat shoe.*

                                    Fig.

Fig. K. L. ———— *a leg, the foot supposed to be shod with a convex shoe.*

Fig. No. 7. ———— *a patten or scate shoe.*

Fig. No. 8. ———— *another sort of patten shoe.*

PLATE II.

Fig. M. *Represents the inferior surface of a good foot, having never received any damage from the Farrier.*

Fig. N. ———— *the inferior surface of the foot, whose natural shape has been destroyed by bad shoeing.*

Fig. No. 9. *Represents the hinge or joint shoe, for all feet, with a flat rivet nail joining them together in the toe, so that it may be made both wider and narrower to serve any foot; and with a double range of holes.*

Fig. 10. ———— *the mules shoe for the fore feet, called in French,* planche.

Fig. 11. ———— *the mules shoe for the hind feet, called in French,* florentine.

Fig. 12. ———— *the shoe for an ox.*

An Explanation of the Six Hoofs moulded in Plaister.

No. 1. *Represents a good hoof.*

No. 2. ———— *a hoof bound.*

No. 3. ———— *a flat foot.*

No. 4. ———— *a pommel, or convex foot.*

No. 5. ———— *a crooked foot.*

No. 6. ———— *a foot destroyed by the buttress.*

An

An Explanation of the Six Brass Shoes.

No. 1. *Represents a concave shoe for a good foot.*
No. 2. ———— *a shoe for a good hind foot.*
No. 3. ———— *a shoe for a flat foot.*
No. 4. ———— *a shoe for a convex foot.*
No. 5. ———— *a French shoe.*
No. 6. ———— *a half moon shoe.*

CONTENTS.

CONTENTS.

Of

LECTURE II.

LECTURE III.

Of

LECTURE IV.

LECTURE V.

LECTURE VI.

Proofs

☞ AS, in the course of the following Work, but little has been said concerning the Running Thrush, the Reader is desired to observe, that that disease being of the same nature as the Grease, the Author proposes to treat of it fully, in a Work which will speedily be offered to the Public.

THE AUTHOR of the following sheets is obliged to have recourse again to the candour and indulgence he has so often experienced, on account of the inaccuracies in the printing; but he trusts, that the Reader's justice will make him sensible of the great difficulty attending the printing a work in translation, in a language with which the Author is not yet critically acquainted; especially during the exercise of a very active office; and of the still greater difficulty of finding a person sufficiently interested in the success of a work, to correct the impression with the exactness required. The Reader is earnestly requested to correct the text by the following *errata*, as some of the errors materially affect the sense.

ERRATA.

Page	Line		Page	Line	
9	15	*for* fate *read* fall.	62	14	*for* within, outwardly *read* within outwardly,
10	4	— Gasper *read* Gesner.	65	6	— tic *read* lie.
12	13	— Ben Calann *read* Ben Calaun.	67	14	— for *read* on.
ib.	17	— al sanatrin *read* al sanatein.	74	(note)	— dele the less.
14	11	— excited *read* exerted.	86	24	— five points *read* four points.
19	11	— selected of *read* selected out of.	100	13	— fruition *read* friction.
22	14	— the castle *read* the castle of Alfort.	107	7	— pricker *read* picker.
29	7	— 40 livres *read* 40 lou:s.	10	19	— require *read* acquire.
34	20	— vice-precident *read* vice-president.	118	13	— close *read* lose.
39	15	— two parts *read* two ducts.	119	18	— he's *read* he is.
41	18	— 1765 *read* 1665.	121	10	— No. 1 *read* No. 6.
49		— ferrare (note) *read* ferrure.	138	8	— elaboratory *read* elaborate.
54	18	— and *read* or.	148	12	— conjecture *read* conjuncture.
59	1	— heals *read* heels.	167	1	— retisulng *read* resulting.

Table of the Geometrical Proportions of Eclipse.

THE head divided into 22 equal parts is the common measure for every part of the body. If the head appears too long or too short in a horse, that common measure must be abandoned, and the height of the body taken from the top of the withers to the ground. This height being divided into three equal parts, one of these three parts sub-divided into 22 equal parts will give a just geometrical length, such as the head would have given had it been rightly proportioned.

AAAC. 3 heads and 13 parts give the height of Eclipse, when properly placed, from the foretop to the ground.

AAA. 3 heads, from the withers to the ground.

AAA. 3 heads, from the rump to the ground.

E   AAA.

AAA. 3 heads and 3 parts, the whole length of the body, from the most prominent part of the chest to the extremity of the buttocks.

AAA. 2 heads and 20 parts, the height of the middle of the body, through the line of the centre of gravity.

AAC. 2 heads and 7 parts, the height of the highest part of the chest from the ground.

AAC. 2 heads and 5 parts, the height of the perpendicular line, which falls from the articulation of the arm with the shoulder, directly to the hoof.

AB. 1 head and 20 parts, the height of the perpendicular line, which falls from the top of the fore leg, dividing equally all its parts to the fetlock.

AB. 1 head and 19 parts, the height of the perpendicular line from the elbow to the ground.

AB. 1 head and 19 parts, the distance from the top of the withers to the stifle. The same measure also gives the distance from the top of the rump to the elbow.

A. 1½ head, the length of the neck from the withers to the top of the head. The same measure also gives the length of the neck, from the top of the head to its insertion into the chest

A. 1 head, the width of the neck at its union with the chest.

D. 12 parts of a head, the width of the neck in its narrowest part.

D. The same measure gives the breadth of the head, taken below the eyes.

A. 1 head and 4 parts, the thickness of the body from the middle of the back to the middle of the belly.

E 2   A. The

A. The same measure gives the breadth of the body.

A. The same measure gives the length of the rump, from its summit to the extremity of the buttocks.

A. The same measure gives the distance from the root of the tail to the articulation of the femur with the tibia, commonly called the stifle.

A. The same measure gives the length from the stifle to the hock.

A. The same measure gives the height, from the hock to the extremity of the hoof.

B. 20 parts of a head, the distance from the extremity of the buttocks to the articulation of the stifle.

B. The same measure gives the breadth of the rump or croup.

E. 10 parts of a head, the breadth of the fore legs from their anterior part to the elbow.

F. 10 parts of a head, the breadth of one of the hind legs, taken beneath the fold of the buttocks.

F. 8 parts of a head, the breadth of the ham taken from the bend.

F. The same measure gives the breadth of the head above the nostrils.

G. 7 parts of a head, the distance of the eyes, from one great angle to the other.

G. The same measure gives the distance between the fore legs.

H. 5 parts of a head, the thickness of the knees.

H. The

H. The same measure gives the breadth of the fore legs, above the knees.

H. The same measure gives the thickness of the hams.

I. 4 parts of a head, the breadth of the pastern or fetlock joint.

I. The same measure gives the thickness of the coronet.

K. 4¼ parts of a head, the breadth of the coronet.

L. 3 parts of a head, the thickness of the fore legs in their narrowest part.

L. The same measure gives the breadth of the hinder legs, or shanks.

M. 2¼ parts of a head, the thickness of the hind pasterns.

M. The same measure gives the breadth of the shanks of the fore legs.

N. $2\frac{1}{4}$ parts of a head, the thickness of the fore pasterns.

N. The same measure gives the breadth of the hind pasterns.

O. $1\frac{3}{4}$ parts of a head, the thickness of the fore and hind shanks.

Perpendicular Lines in Eclipse's Fore Legs.

AAC. The first perpendicular line has been already described; it falls from the articulation of the arm with the shoulder, precisely to the edge of the toe. This line ought not to deviate from this direction.

AC. The second perpendicular line falls from the middle of the breast directly to the middle point of the space which separates the two fore feet.

A. The third perpendicular line falls from the middle of the knee, and divides in equal parts all the pieces which compose the rest of the extremity, to the ground.

AB. The fourth perpendicular line falls from the top of the side of the fore legs, and divides equally all the parts to the pastern.

Perpendicular Lines in his Hind Legs.

AA. The first line falls perpendicularly from the articulation of the stifle to the ground, and should touch the ground at the distance of half a head from the toe.

A. The second falls from above the bend of the ham, exactly to the hoof.

A. The

Anatomical G

A. The third falls from the point of the hock, and divides in equal parts all the rest of the leg, to the ground.

A. The fourth falls from the middle of the buttocks, exactly to the middle point of the space, which separates the hind feet.

All these perpendicular lines, which existed really in Eclipse, as may be seen in his skeleton, constituted the most beautiful and important quality of his structure. These same lines may serve as rules in the choice of the best race-horses.

Explanation of the second Plate, which represents the Motions of the Legs of Eclipse.

HEIGHT AND LENGTH OF ECLIPSE.

Inches.

The height from the withers to the ground 66

F . The

Inches.

The height from the top of the rump to the
ground   -   -   -   -   67

Length of the body, taken from the most
prominent part of the breast to the extremity
of the buttocks   -   -   -   . 69

Length of the Bones which compose the Legs.

FORE LEGS.	In.	HIND LEGS.	In.
A. The shoulder blade - -	18	G. The os-ileon - - -	12
B. The humerus or arm - -	12	H. The femur - - -	15
C. The cubitus or fore arm -	16	I. The tibia - - - -	19
D. The canon or shank - -	12	K. The shank or leg - -	14
E. The pastern, the coronet, and foot - - - -	7	L. The pastern, the coronet, and foot - - - -	9

Extent of Flexion in the Parts which compose the Extremities.

F. All the lines which proceed horizontally
and obliquely from the centre to the circumference

ence of each circle, and on which is the letter F, mark the extent of flexion, either forward or backward.

The Fore Legs.

A. The shoulder describes a portion of a circle, equal to 40 degrees, both forward and backward; the centre of its motion being in the middle of the shoulder blade.

B. The humerus, or arm, is represented in the the centre of flexion backward; it describes 40 degrees in its action.

C. The cubitus, or fore arm, is represented at the beginning of its flexion forward, and describes 90 degrees in its action.

D. The shank, or canon, is at the beginning of its flexion backward, and describes 90 degrees in its action.

F 2

E. The pastern, coronet, and foot, describe, one with another, in their flexion backward, 100 degrees.

RECAPITULATION.

	Degrees.
A	- - - - - - - 40
B	- - - - - - - 40
C	- - - - - - - 90
D	- - - - - - - 90
E	- - - - - - 100

Total of the flexion 360

Hind Legs.

G. The haunch, or os ileon, bends upward and downward, and describes 30 degrees in its action.

H. The

H. The femur, or thigh bone, is represented in the middle of its flexion forward, and describes 50 degrees.

I. The tibia is represented in one third of its flexion backward, and describes in the whole 80 degrees.

K. The shank is represented in the beginning of its flexion forward, and describes 100 degrees.*

L. The pastern, coronet, and foot, describe, one with another, 100 degrees.

RECAPITULATION.

		Degrees.
G	- - - - - - - -	3 0
H	- - - - - - - -	5 0
I	- - - - - - - -	8 0
K	- - - - - - -	10 0
L	- - - - - - -	10 0

Total of the flexion 360

* The line of flexion of this part is not placed sufficiently high in the plate.

We may see by this, that the legs of Eclipse, in their flexion in the gallop, described each a circle of 360 degrees; and, consequently, the extent of the action of each leg was the same in the extension.

To this must be added the force of action, without which an horse cannot even walk. This force depends chiefly on the power of the muscles, and can only be computed by experiment; since they are animated organs, which move parts merely mechanical : but, in allowing Eclipse a good muscular organization, which he certainly possessed, we may, examining the length and direction of his legs, and the greatness and openness of the angles, formed by the alternate disposition of the bones which composed his extremities, pronounce with the greatest probability, that Eclipse, free of all weight, and galloping at liberty in his greatest speed, could cover an extent of 25 feet at each complete action on the gallop; that he could repeat this action twice and one third in each

each second; consequently, that, employing without reserve all his natural and mechanical faculties on a straight line, he could run nearly four miles in the space of six minutes and two seconds.

HF. These two letters placed in the four prints of the feet, which are marked before and behind the horse's legs, shew where he placed his hind and fore feet in the gallop.

Lines of Progression.

M. The great segment of a circle, which proceeds from the print of one of the hind feet, and enters the print of one of the fore feet, shews the total extent of ground which the horse covered at each complete action in the gallop.

N. The oblique line, which proceeds from the protuberance of the hip bone, and meets the print

of

of the first hind foot, shews the total extent, and the force of action, of the hind legs.

O. The second oblique line, which proceeds in the same manner from the point of the hip, and meets one of the prints of the fore feet, shews the position of the hind foot when it presses the ground in the act of galloping.

P. The third oblique line, which proceeds from the summit of the shoulder, and meets one of the prints of the fore feet, shews the extent and force of action in the fore legs.

Q. The fourth oblique line, which proceeds from the shoulder, and meets the last print of the hind feet, shews the spot from whence the fore foot rises in the progression, until its action is finished.

R. The two curve lines which proceed, the one from the hoof of the fore foot, and the other

from

from the hoof of the hind foot, mark simply the compass of the extension of the four legs.

THE speed of Eclipse being a fact established, and well ascertained, the excellence of his construction should naturally be admitted. The velocity of his gallop could only result from the harmonious combination in the organs of progression. Let us now suppose these same organs faulty by any defect in their proportions, and let us now inquire what would be the consequence. We will begin with the head.

Defect in the Proportion of the Head.

The body, neck, and head of a horse, may be considered as forming a large lever, whose fulcrum is in the fore legs. The head, being joined to the extremity of the anterior arm of this lever, formed by the neck, must necessarily counterpoise some

G part

part of the posterior arm, formed by the body.
If the head is too short, the evil will not indeed
be very great, but the counterpoise will be unequal ; the hinder part will be obliged to exert
more strength to determine the weight of the
body forwards ; the fore-hand will be lighter,
but it will be at the expence of the progression.
The fault will be more considerable if the head
be too long and heavy, because it will in that case
overweigh that portion of the hind quarter, unto
which it should only equiponderate : the fore-
legs being overcharged, will detach themselves
from the ground with the less facility, will continue raised in their elevation a shorter time, and
will cover less ground in their advance.

Defect in the Proportion of the Neck.

The faults of the neck are in general the consequences of the defects of the head ; for it is an
uncommon thing to see a short head with a long
neck,

neck, as, on the contrary, to see a long head with a short neck.

If the neck is too short, the fault will be an addition to that of a too short head. The case will be the same if the neck is too long; for the head will naturally weigh heavier, in proportion as it is removed from the fulcrum or rest of the lever, supposing it to be well proportioned. Its length, as has been shewn in the table, should be nearly one third of the height of the body, measuring from the withers to the ground. The neck will be well proportioned if it measures one head and a half from the nape to the withers.

Defect of Proportion in the Height of the Body, from the Withers to the Ground.

The fore-hand of a horse only appears low in relation to his hind quarter; for it is as allowable to say that a horse is high behind, as to say that

G 2   he

he is low before ; particularly in the general figure of horses.   But since it is proved, that animals which Nature has designed for speed have
more extent in their hind than in their fore parts;
I should not consider it as a fault in a race-horse,
if the withers lay below an horizontal line drawn
from the rump, provided the difference should
not exceed an inch and a half, or two inches ;
if it exceeded this, the hind legs would impel the
body with too much force upon the fore legs ;
and the weight falling at each pace upon the fore
legs in an oblique direction would overload them,
and retard their action.   This fault would be increased, if the head was too voluminous and the
neck too long.

If the withers were higher than the rump, there
would result a contrary effect to the preceding,
but which equally tend to retard the progression,
since the hind legs would be obliged to overcome
the resistance of the body in an oblique direction
upwards ; this is an uncommon fault.   Whether
the

the horse be too low or too high before, the rider may restore him to the equilibrium so necessary for the freedom of translation, by bringing the centre of gravity of his own body, before or behind the centre of gravity of his horse's body. By thus reasoning his seat, he may lessen the defect which a blind practice cannot fail to increase. It is not sufficient merely to increase or lessen the weight which horses are to carry, in order to establish an equality between themselves, or to equalize their speed; it is necessary to make a just division and distribution of the weight upon each separate individual. The rider should likewise reason well all his motions and actions; for the least of them is capable of producing a sensible effect. A quarter of a second becomes an important division of time in a race. None better know its value than they who lose or win by the length of half a head.

Defect

Defect in the Length of the Body.

The measure of Eclipse's body, taken from the extremity of the buttocks to the chest, proves that a race-horse is not to be contained within a perfect square, since the length of his body exceeded its height nearly by one tenth.

If the body were longer, the loins would be too flexible and weak ; their vigour depends upon their shortness ; for the vertebræ of the loins are thus closer to each other, and intimately united by shorter ligaments : the muscles which move them are also stronger, being shorter and thicker. A horse thus constructed would be unpleasant in the manage ; but what is there considered as a fault, becomes a requisite and essential quality in a race-horse.

The firmness of the loins of English horses, the little freedom of their shoulders, a passion for

riding fast over a level country, and the impossi-
bility of sustaining a long journey without rising
from the saddle, are the reasons, resulting from
necessity, which directed to the first principles of
English horsemanship ; principles which it is my
design to examine in a future work.

Shortness of the Body.

When the body of a horse is too short, the column of the spine is naturally stiff and inflexible.
The motion of the loins is so much confined, that
the vertebræ of the back and loins appear to
compose but one piece. The quadrilatural figure,
formed by the four legs, is reduced, through the
approach of the hinder to the fore extremities.
In this position the limbs have less power of extension, both backward and forward ; and there
results a real loss to the progression.

Natural

Natural Direction of the Back and Loins.

The spine, which reaches from the withers to the rump, should describe an horizontal line. For this purpose, it is necessary that the points of which it is composed (that is to say the vertebræ of the back) should unite by surfaces vertically cut ; the whole is then complete, and the pressure of the hind legs against so well-constructed a column is communicated to all its parts, and produces at the same moment of time an entire removal of the whole line from its first station forward.

Of the Bending of the Back inwards.

If the column of which we have just spoken is bent inwards, we say that the horse is hollow or saddle backed. If it is bent outwards, we say that

that he is ass-backed. In the former case, the animal is never securely strong; the muscles labour even in a state of inaction; the weight of the viscera of the lower belly serves to increase the bend of the spine; the rump is unsteady in its paces; and the pressure of the hinder extremities rather tends, in its immediate effect, to unite the two extreme points of the spine, by displacing the intermediate ones. This faulty construction, then, evidently retards progression, since the fore part of the animal receives but slowly and feebly the effect of the action of the hinder part.

Of the Bending of the Back outwards.

The shortness of the body only brings the four legs nearer to each other, but does not any way impair their perpendicular; whereas the outward curvature of the spine not only brings the four legs nearer to each other, but gives them more-

H   over

over an oblique direction, which diminishes the stability of the machine, and abridges the paces of the horse; because the hind leg is obliged to leave the ground as soon as it has attained its perpendicular; while in a horse, whose position is good, the space which the legs describe extends from the oblique forward, through the perpendicular, to the oblique backward.

The opposite conformation to this is, where the four extremities are too distant from each other: in this case, the horse is defective in speed, inasmuch as the hind legs effect their extension, counting only from the perpendiculars.

Defect resulting from the Size of the Body.

The body of Eclipse, measured through, from the middle of the back to the middle of the belly, was one head and four parts in depth, as it is marked in the table of his proportions. But this

would

would be too much in a young race-horse. It must be remembered, that when this measure was taken Eclipse was twenty-six years old, and that he was, of course, become more corpulent than in his youth.

The bulk of the belly does not only increase the weight of the mass, but incommodes also the action of the hind legs, which cannot attain the central point of the body. This fault is rare among race-horses, most of which are remarkable for the opposite defect.

Defect proceeding from too spare a Body.

The primary cause of the goodness of any horse must be the exact and regular performance of all the functions necessary to his system. A good organization of the viscera should then correspond to a good conformation of the outward parts. If, for example, the organs destined to digestion and

H 2   chilifica-

chilification are in a state of weakness and debility, the aliments will be ill digested, the chyle
ill prepared, the nutrition imperfect, the whole
system languid, and the horse will be incapable of
sustaining violent races, which strain and try his
wind.   A belly that is too thin, and confined
in the flanks, containing intestines of too in-
considerable a bulk, would subject the animal to
all these evil consequences.   I therefore think,
that the body of a race-horse should be in the
proporion of about twenty parts of a head ; and
I entreat proprietors of horses to make trial of
this rule, in order to ascertain whether it be in
harmony with Nature.

Defects in the Proportion of the Thorax or Chest.

Freedom and length in breathing, are qualities as
essential to a race-horse as a good conformation
in his limbs.   If the capacity of the chest is in-
considerable, the viscera which they contain will
be

be constrained in the performance of their functions. The blood, whose rapidity increases with
exercise, will find its passage through the lungs
with greater or less difficulty; the breathing will
become shorter, and more accelerated; the animal will lose his wind; his legs will grow weak
under him; and even suffocation may ensue, if
he is imprudently urged beyond the limits of the
vital powers which Nature has given him.

When the chest is too narrow, there follows a
defect in the fore legs, which are by this means
brought too near each other. This position renders them unfirm and wavering, and deprives the
horse of confidence in his fore-hand; besides,
that a horse thus constructed is liable to the
pulmonaria. This disorder first discovers itself
by leanness, copious sweats, and a continued
diarrhœa.

A too capacious chest would be also a defect
in a race-horse, by increasing the weight of the
body,

body, and surcharging the fore legs : but if I had to choose between two horses, one of whom should have rather a large chest, and the other too narrow a one, I should decide in favour of the former; especially, if he was otherwise well organized in his limbs. The chest of Eclipse was singularly well made and proportioned.

It would nevertheless be possible to turn to account a horse whose chest should not enjoy all the capacity required, by moderating his exercises, and proportioning their duration to his powers. By following this method, the organs of breathing might be gradually accustomed to a greater labour, but always in relation and subjection to the primitive constitution of the individual.

If the fact prove, that the habits of a moderate exercise is capable of improving respiration, there can be no doubt but that this function, when in its perfection, may on the other hand sustain speed : if it can do it but for the space of a second

cond only, the end will be gained; since it does not even require that short space of time to render a horse useful or injurious to the interests of his master.

Trainers of horses, versed in the mysteries of their art, will, no doubt, pass hastily over my physical observations; but I hope that persons acquainted with the organization of the animal œconomy will condescend to stop, a little while at least, to examine them.

Of the Croup or Rump.

The size of the croup of Eclipse, as it is given in the table of his proportions, always has appeared to me too great; and the examination of the ileon bones has confirmed me, in that opinion. The extent of the os pubis and ischion occasioned too great a distance between the hind legs; so that two lines drawn from the fore to the hind feet,

instead

instead of running parallel to each other, incline outward. This defect necessarily occasioned a degree of wavering in the croup, perceptible, and somewhat unpleasant, in his gallop; but the muscular powers of the animal in question over-ruled the little defects which subsisted in the mechanism of his skeleton. When the croup is too narrow, the muscles which communicate with the loins and extremities are thin, and consequently weak. It is easily conceived, that such an organization is a great fault in a race-horse.

FORE LEGS.

Of the Shoulder and Arm.

It would be needless to repeat here, the observations which I made on the mechanism of the shoulder, in the beginning of this essay; I will only add, that this part was too much loaded in Eclipse. It ought not, however, to be too

spare;

spare; because the muscles would then be weak, and the motions of the shoulder-blade confined.

The proportions of the arm, or humerus, is commonly determined by that of the shoulder-blade. These two parts, forming together the sides of an angle, more or less open, give to the muscles, which move them, a greater or less power, in proportion as they remove them farther from, or bring them nearer to, the axis of motion.

Of the Fore-arm, or Radius.

The breadth of the fore-arm, being the effect of the bulk of the muscles which encompass the radius, indicates its strength in action. The extent of this action is the produce of the length of the part in question; for, supposing it to be freely jointed, it is evident that a radius of sixteen inches long will, in its progress forward, describe a portion of a larger circle than one that is shorter.

I

The

The length of the fore-arm is then of great avail to the speed of progression. This part was well proportioned in Eclipse.

Of the Leg, or Shank.

In proportion as the fore-arm is long, the leg or shank will be short. The shortness and breadth of this part secures its strength : if it is too thick, it is strong, but clumsy ; if it is long and thin, it is weak ; but the case is not the same if it be wide ; because the force of the muscles will increase, in proportion as the tendon or sinew is removed from the centre of motion. I apprehend that a horse will be exempt from all reproach, who shall be made in this part like Eclipse. See the table of proportions.

Of the Pastern, Coronet, and Foot.

The pastern, coronet, and foot, bending in the same direction, and describing one line from the fetlock

fetlock to the ground, may be considered as forming together one piece.

A column possesses all its possible strength
when placed perpendicularly ; its stability is impaired in proportion as it is made to deviate from
that direction. It should appear then, at first
sight, that Nature had neglected the solidity and
stability of the edifice, in giving an oblique direction to the basis of the four columns destined
to support it. But her industry and wisdom are
easily discernible in the sructure of those beings
which she has gifted with the faculty of translation, since that faculty could not have effect,
without the aid of those angles, whose number
and extension determine the speed, in the displacing and translation of the body.

Not only the alternate angular disposition of
the bony pieces which compose the columns, assist progression ; but they also secure the viscera
of the chest and lower belly from the shocks

I 2
which

which they must infallibly have sustained, had
the percussion on the ground taken place perpendicularly. The angles, more or less removed
from this direction, are so many springs lessening
the effect of re-action. Thus, the obliquity of
the pastern, coronet, and foot, wonderfully favour
the views of Nature. This obliquity, however,
may be too great or too small, according to the
use which we wish to make of the horse.

Too long a pastern increases the flexibility
of the fetlock, but lessens the leg. Horses
thus constructed are extremely pliant and sup-
ple; they are much admired in the manage,
because they communicate little re-action to
the rider. But this elegance would become
a fault in a race-horse; in which we require
strength and solidity in the parts of which we are
speaking. A shorter pastern, whose bulk is in
proportion to the rest of the leg, will better sustain the weight of the body, and more strongly
resist the re-action from the ground.

When

When the pastern is too short, the animal is almost direct upon his legs. This faulty position lessens the stability of his fore-hand, and renders him liable to fall at each step. An anatomical knowledge of the parts of which the leg is composed, will qualify us to judge of their relative proportions.

Eclipse having been foundered many years previous to his death, his fore feet were much disfigured. The havock made by this disorder having changed the direction both of the coronet and pastern, it was not possible for me to determine with precision the proportions of these parts. Briefly, our knowledge of horses must be very limited, if we are not capable of judging whether a horse is too long or too short jointed.

HIND LEGS.

Of the Thigh.

The parts which composed the hind extremity of Eclipse were remarkable for their length.

The femur formed with the os ileon a considerable angle, whence followed a great extent of motion. The length of the tibia gave a most beautiful proportion to the leg. The hock, through its width, possessed great strength, and its elastic quality or spring must necessarily have produced the greatest possible degree of extension. The leg or shank, the pastern, coronet and foot, corresponded to the good conformation of the upper part of the member. The proportions of each part may be seen in the table, and compared with those of a horse of the height of Eclipse.

Of the Perpendicular.

If we were to deny the necessity of a perpendicular position of the parts destined to the support of an animal body, we should openly arraign the laws established by Nature. The perpendicular not only insures the stability of the structure, by the exact arrangement of the bones one upon

the

the other, and by an equal distribution of the weight upon each, but it also favours progression, by maintaining a perfect equability in the projection of the mass. When the legs are in action, each one receiving only its due share of the weight, and always in the perpendicular line, transfers its burthen to its neighbour with ease. The weight being thus received and sent, advances in proportion to the completion of the action of each leg. But if the perpendicular is disturbed; if the distribution of the weight is unequal; in a word, if any point of the base is overloaded, the harmony between the legs will be destroyed, and the progression will be retarded.

We may thence conclude, that without the perpendicular, the animal could not enjoy the stability required. Let us now see in what this perpendicular consists.

Perpendicular

Perpendicular Lines in Eclipse.

FORE LEGS.

For the convenience of the Reader, I shall re-capitulate the perpendicular lines, according to the order in which they stand in the table of proportions. These lines are nine in number.

The 1st is a line falling perpendicularly from the articulation of the arm with the shoulder, to the toe of the fore foot.

The 2d line falls perpendicularly from the upper part of the fore-arm, or elbow, to the heel of the fore foot ; after having divided longitudinally in its course the fore-arm, knee, and leg or shank.

The 3d falls from a little above the knee, and, dividing the knee into two equal parts, descends along

along the anterior surface of the leg or shank, pastern, coronet, and foot, dividing them also into two equal parts.

The 4th falls from the centre of the chest to the ground, dividing the interval between the two fore legs into two equal parts.

HIND LEGS.

The 5th falls from the stifle, or articulation of the femur with the tibia, to the ground, at the distance of half an head before the toe of the fore foot.

The 6th descends from the point of the hock, or the calcaneum, along the tendon of the hind leg, and, dividing longitudinally the thickness of the shank, fetlock, pastern, coronet, and foot, touches the ground, opposite to the opening of the frog.

K   The

The 7th falls from the centre of the buttocks to the ground, dividing the interval between the two hind legs into two equal parts.

The 8th falls from the withers to the ground, touching the point of the elbow in its course.

The 9th is only the line of the centre of gravity of the horse's body; it falls from the middle of the back, through the body, to the central point of the quadrilateral figure, described by the four legs.

The particular and relative position of the legs of Eclipse were sufficiently perfect to bear the application of the perpendicular lines which I have just described. Had there been any fault in their direction, I should have carefully noticed it in the plate. I will now inquire what are the inconveniences which would result from the interruption of the perpendicular in each particular line.

FORE

FORE LEGS.

Interruption of the Perpendicular in the first Line.

If the foot is placed before the first perpendicular line, the leg will stand obliquely forward; it will cover less ground in its action; the duration of its stay upon the ground will be abridged; the stay, which will be only on the heel, will communicate to the body a kind of repulsion, inimical to progression. In horses of this kind, the fore legs come upon the ground nearly in the direction of those of a horse on the descent.

If the obliquity of the leg is behind the perpendicular line, the animal will be ever on the point of falling; because the foot, being drawn too near the centre of gravity, will have to sustain a larger share of the weight of the body; the bending of the leg will be troublesome, and his paces will be abridged.

Interruption

Interruption in the second Line.

The leg deviates from the second line, by standing before or behind it. The inconvenien-ces which result from this are, therefore, the same as those which we have just described. Some-times this faulty direction originates at the knee, in which case the horse is said to be bow-legged. In either case he must be rejected as a racer.

Interruption in the third Line.

When the lower extremity of the limb exceeds the perpendicular line, the bony parts are ill united ; they do not bear exactly on each other; the distribution of the weight being unequal on every part of the circumference of the foot, the tread is less firm, and the steps more or less con-fined. Commonly, the perpendicular line is only
disturbed

disturbed between the fetlock and the ground. The foot, likewise, is sometimes turned inward, and sometimes outward. These faults, according to their degree, are more or less hurtful to progression.

Interruption in the fourth Line.

The perpendicular can only be interrupted in the fourth line by the knees bending inward ; or by the feet being placed too near to each other, occasioned by the outward inclination of the fore-arms. In the former case, the legs move out of the line of the body, and throw aukwardly, one to the other, the weight which they sustain. From this action results a lateral motion, contrary to that of progression. It is the same, but inversely, with regard to the second case. Moreover, the too near approach of the feet impairs the stability of the horse, and renders it more difficult for him to preserve his balance in action.

HIND

HIND LEGS.

Interruption in the fifth Line.

We have seen in the table of proportions, that the toe of the hind foot of Eclipse was distant half a head from the perpendicular line, which falls from the stifle to the ground. If the feet advance nearer to this line, the hocks must proportionably bend ; the weight of the body will be increased upon them, even in inaction ; the position of the feet being too near the centre of gravity, will render it impossible for them to cover much ground, and their step will be very much confined : the extension of the hock taking place from the perpendicular, will rather occasion the elevation of the body, than aid its advance ; from all which it may be perceived, how much this fault must influence on speed.

If,

If, on the contrary, the hind feet stand too far behind this line, the hocks will be nearly straight; their flexion will be limited; the feet will not be able sufficiently to approach the centre of gravity; they will cover less ground; and the extension of the hinder parts will be partial, taking place only from the perpendicular backward. Thence there must be a loss of speed, relative to the remainder of the spaces which the legs ought to have embraced.

It is commonly thought, that, in the paces of a well-proportioned horse, the hind feet ought never to pass beyond the fore feet. This notion, however, is contradicted in a good race-horse; the extent of the hind quarters of such a horse, and the freedom of their action, convey the hind feet much beyond the centre of gravity; and I conceive this to be true of all animals which Nature has designed for speed.

Interruption

Interruption in the sixth Line.

The same fault in the legs, which interrupts the perpendicular in the fifth line, interrupts it also in the sixth ; consequently, the inconveniences which result are the same.

Interruption in the seventh Line.

When the seventh perpendicular line passes either within or without any of those parts which it ought to divide longitudinally into equal divisions, the perpendicular is evidently disturbed in those parts. Whether the fault exists in the hock, the bones of which, being ill disposed, do not bear equally upon each other ; or whether it originates in the articulation of the fetlock, which is defective from the same cause, the legs lose more or less of their power, because their tread does

does not take place upon the line of the body, and all motion which deviates from that line is a loss to the progression.

Interruption in the eighth Line.

The perpendicular may be disturbed in the eighth line; 1st, by the great breadth of the croup, and the approach of the hind feet to each other: this defect is rare among race horses. 2d. By the femur inclining outward; a direction which affects all the rest of the limb, bringing the hocks together, and turning the feet outward. 3d. The interruption of the perpendicular may begin at the hock; the bones of which, being ill arranged, may determine the joint inward. Whether the hocks bend outward, as in the former case, or whether they bend inward, as in the second and third cases, the leg will not be able to move upon the line of the body. The croup will waver to the right and left; and all the lateral motions will be so much loss from progression. Whatever, then, may be the strength of the loins, and of the other parts, a true and exact perpendicular in the hind legs is of the first degree of importance, since that the slightest interruption in this respect must affect the speed. It is not exactly the same with regard to the fore legs, whose office is rather to sustain the body than to convey it forwards.

The 9th line only determines the proper situation of the withers.

The 10th line is no other than the direction of the centre of gravity of the animal's body.

In judging of the perpendicular in a horse, there is no necessity to have the rule, compass, or hippometer always in the hand ; he who has studied the skeleton, will acquire a sufficient degree of accuracy to satisfy himself of the good or bad position of the legs by surveying them sideways,

ways, in front, and behind; particularly, if he takes good care that the horse be placed on a perfectly level ground.

Those who differ materially from these principles will object to me, no doubt, that all race-horses are not cast in the same mould; that they are not all shaped exactly alike; and, consequently, that the same rule cannot be applied indiscriminately to all. I answer, that the difference which they think they see between two horses whose speed is nearly equal, can only deceive those whose knowledge does not extend below the outward surface of the body. Even the difference of colour may do away, to the eye, the identity of proportions; but he who is well acquainted with the construction and mechanism of the organs of progression, will not allow himself to be deceived by the first appearance. He will discover, and recognize a conformity, in parts which at the first sight appeared to him en-

tirely

tirely dissimulation. I acknowledge, however, that a great disparity in the natural constitution of individuals, may sometimes weaken the force of my observations; but it can never entirely destroy it.

There can be no doubt, but that of two horses of the same size, the one may be speedier than the other, because the texture of the organs may be compact and close in the one, and weak and relaxed in the other; but this exception cannot affect the general rules which I have laid down in the course of this essay. These rules can direct a great way in the choice of a race-horse; they may also save any one much trouble and anxiety, who is fruitlessly endeavouring to exact from a young horse a degree of speed which Nature has refused him. I entreat proprietors of studs to impress themselves with these observations; to apply them to colts at least a year old; and to convince themselves, by experience, whether or no they comprise any useful truths.

Six

Six complete Actions of the Gallop.

PLATE II.

This plate represents six complete actions of the gallop of Eclipse; each action covers twenty-five feet. The six actions, marked with the figures 1, 2, 3, 4, 5, 6, offer a scale of 150 feet.

It is well known to all who have observed the action of the horse, that the gallop consists of a repetition of bounds or leaps, more or less high, and more or less extended, in proportion to the strength and lightness of the animal.

The common gallop contains three *times*. If the horse, for example, begins his gallop on the right, the left hind foot beats the first time; the right hind foot and left fore foot beat the second time together; and the right fore foot beats the third.

In

In the gallop of four *times*, the feet strike the ground in the same order as in walking. Supposing the horse galloping on the right, the left hind foot beats the first time, the right hind foot beats the second, the left fore foot beats the third, and the right fore foot beats the fourth. This gallop is regular, but confined, and but little adapted for speed.

The gallop at two *times* is faster than that at three, or at four; the legs follow in the same order as in the trot; so that the two sounds are given by the left hind foot and right fore foot striking the ground together, and by the right hind foot and left fore foot all striking the ground together.

Explanation

Explanation of Plate III.

Fig. I. Represents a very broad hock.

A. The tibia.

B. The shank.

C. The calcaneum.

DD. The two lines which proceed from the centre of the joint, form the sides of the angle of the hock.

E. The portion of the circle contained between the two extremities of the two branches of the angle, shews the openness of the angle of the hock. This angle contains 40 degrees.

F. The union of the two branches of the angle, at the centre of the joint of the hock.

Fig. II. Represents a hock, somewhat smaller than the preceding.

A. The tibia.

B. The canon.

C. The

C. The calcaneum.

DD. The two branches of the angle of the hock.

E. The portion of the circle contained between the two extremities of the two branches of the angle, shews the openness of the angle of the hock. This angle only contains 30 degrees.

F. The union of the two branches of the angle, at the centre of the joint of the hock.

Fig. III. Represents a very long shoulder, and in a very oblique direction.

A. The shoulder-blade.

B. The arm or humerus.

CC. The perpendicular line which marks the extent of the motion of the shoulder.

DD. The centrical line of the shoulder-blade.

EE. The two parts of a circle which the shoulder describes, forward, backward, upward, and downward. These portions contain each 40 degrees.

Fig.

Fig. IV. Represents a shoulder as long as the former, but in a less oblique direction.

A. The shoulder-blade.

B. The arm or humerus.

CC. A perpendicular line, which marks the extent of the motions of the shoulder.

DD. The centrical line of the shoulder-blade.

EE. The two portions of a circle which the shoulder describes, forward, backward, upward, and downward. These portions contain only 30 degrees each.

THE END.

M

PEDIGREE OF ECLIPSE.

THIS famous horse belonged to Mr. O'Kelly : was bred by the late Duke of Cumberland ; and bought by Mr. Wildman, out of His Royal Highness's stud, at a public sale of some of his horses, for 46 guineas : who afterwards sold him to Mr. O'Kelly for 1700 guineas. In 1769 he won the 50 guineas sweep-stakes, and the 50l. plate at Epsom ; 50l. at Ascot Heath ; the King's plate, and the 50l. plate at Winchester ; the 100 guineas ; the cup ; and 30 guineas at Salisbury ; and the King's plate at Canterbury, Lewes, and Litchfield. In 1779 he received 600 guineas forfeit at Newmarket, and also won the King's plate ; the King's plate also at Guildford, Nottingham, and York ; also 319l. 10s. at the latter place ; the King's plate at Lincoln ; and again at Newmarket ; as also 150 guineas, besides many other considerable sums. He was never outrun.

Eclipse was got by Mask, son of Squirt ; who was begot by Bartlet's Childers ; his Dam was begot by Regulus ; his grand-dam, by a brother of the whole blood of Wildman's Squirrel ; his great grand-dam by Lord Darcey's Montague; his great great grand-dam by Hautboy ; and his great great great grand-dam by Brimmer, the son of Oglethorpe's Arabian.

He died Feb. 27, 1789, in the 26th year of his age.

A Letter *from M. Broussonet*, M. D. *perpetual Secretary to the Royal Society of Agriculture in Paris, and Fellow of the Royal Society of London, to Mr. Sainbel.*

(TRANSLATION)

Paris, March 16, 1790.

SIR,

THE two letters which you have done me the honour to write, and the box which contained the engravings of Eclipse, have reached me safe. I should not have delayed so long to thank you, nor to acknowledge the reception of them, but that I intended to have conveyed you the same by means of a friend who at that time was about to depart for London, but who has since altered his mind. Have the goodness, my dear Sir, to accept my best thanks for the packet that you have had the kindness to send to me. The explanation which you give of the move-

ments

ments of the horse appears to me extremely inte-
resting and proper to give an advantageous idea of
veterinary knowledge in a country where that art
has not yet been practised upon principle.   In-
closed you will find, Sir, the letter which you desired me to write to Sir Joseph Banks.   And I have
likeways sent another letter in your favour to another of my friends, Dr. Smith.   I shall be extremely
happy to hear that your situation in London is in
every respect agreeable to you ; and it will be ever
the highest satisfaction to me if I can in any measure contribute to it.

I have the honour to be, with the sincerest attachment,

Sir,

Your very humble and

Very obedient Servant,

BROUSSONET.

FRONTISPIECE.

a L'afpect de La Vérité
La Routine S'etonne, L'ignorance S'enfuit.

London. Printed for Martin & Bain. Fleet Street. May 1 1795.

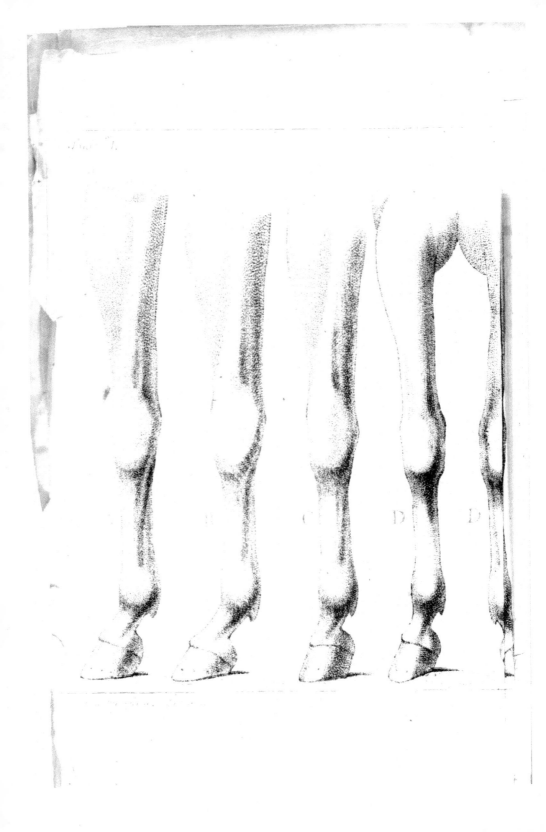

Plate 2.

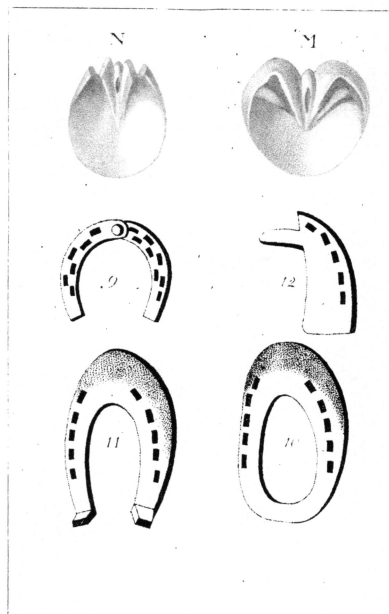

Drawn by R. Lawrence. Engraved by R. Scott.

Plate III.

HOOFS.

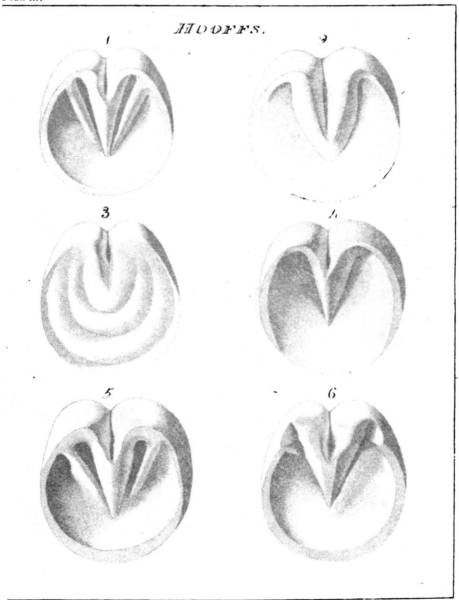

London.Printed for Martin & Bain.Fleet Street.May 1.1795.

Plate IV.

SHOES.

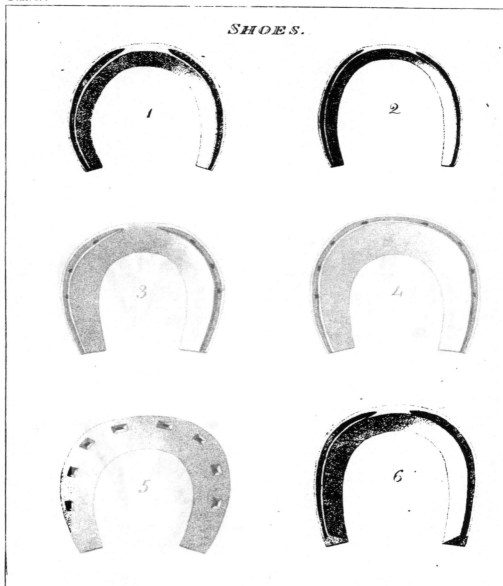

London. Printed for Martin & Bain. Fleet Street. May 1. 1796.

Check Out More Titles From HardPress Classics Series In this collection we are offering thousands of classic and hard to find books. This series spans a vast array of subjects – so you are bound to find something of interest to enjoy reading and learning about.

Subjects:
Architecture
Art
Biography & Autobiography
Body, Mind &Spirit
Children & Young Adult
Dramas
Education
Fiction
History
Language Arts & Disciplines
Law
Literary Collections
Music
Poetry
Psychology
Science
…and many more.

Visit us at www.hardpress.net

Im The Story
personalised classic books

"Beautiful gift.. lovely finish.
My Niece loves it, so precious!"

Helen R Brumfieldon

UNIQUE GIFT

FOR KIDS, PARTNERS
AND FRIENDS

Timeless books such as:

Kids

Alice in Wonderland · The Jungle Book · The Wonderful Wizard of Oz
Peter and Wendy · Robin Hood · The Prince and The Pauper
The Railway Children · Treasure Island · A Christmas Carol

Adults

Romeo and Juliet · Dracula

| Highly Customizable | Change Book's Title | Replace Characters Names & Stories | Upload Photo for inside pages | Add Inscriptions |

Visit
Im The Story.com
and order yours today!

CPSIA information can be obtained
at www.ICGtesting.com
Printed in the USA
BVHW090904280819
556854BV00004B/625/P

9 780461 549454